Pedro Almodóvar

Contemporary Film Directors
Edited by James Naremore

The Contemporary Film Directors series provides concise, well-written introductions to directors from around the world and from every level of the film industry. Its chief aims are to broaden our awareness of important artists, to give serious critical attention to their work, and to illustrate the variety and vitality of contemporary cinema. Contributors to the series include an array of internationally respected critics and academics. Each volume contains an incisive critical commentary, an informative interview with the director, and a detailed filmography.

*A list of books in the series appears
at the end of this book.*

Pedro Almodóvar

Marvin D'Lugo

UNIVERSITY
OF
ILLINOIS
PRESS
URBANA
AND
CHICAGO

1 2 3 4 5 C P 5 4 3 2 1

Library of Congress Cataloging-in-Publication Data

D'Lugo, Marvin, 1943–
Pedro Almodóvar / Marvin D'Lugo.
p.   cm. — (Contemporary film directors)
Includes bibliographical references and index.
ISBN-13: 978-0-252-03117-5 (cloth : alk. paper)
ISBN-10: 0-252-03117-2 (cloth : alk. paper)
ISBN-13: 978-0-252-07361-8 (pbk. : alk. paper)
ISBN-10: 0-252-07361-4 (pbk. : alk. paper)
1. Almodóvar, Pedro—Criticism and interpretation.
I. Title. II. Series.
PN1998.3.A46D58   2006
791.4302'33092—dc22   2005031442

Frontispiece: Pedro Almodóvar, courtesy of El Deseo S.A.

Contents |

Acknowledgments |

This book is the product of more than a decade of discussion, debate, and reflections on the evolution of Pedro Almodóvar's cinema. I am fortunate to have been able to engage in a stimulating intellectual exchange in Spain and the United States with friends and colleagues who listened patiently to my ideas and challenged me to further question critical assumptions about Almodóvar's cinema. Principal among these are José Luis Borau and Román Gubern, both of whom led me to consider subtle and often overlooked aspects of Almodóvar's relation to Spanish and world cinemas. Very special thanks must also go to Marsha Kinder and Kathleen Vernon, with whom I've spent years debating and analyzing Almodóvar's films. The originality and freshness of their approaches to Spanish cinema generally and Almodóvar in particular have provided a continual inspiration and model for my own work.

A debt of gratitude is owed to the family of friends at El Deseo who generously provided important archival access to press materials and helped me throughout the development of this book. Special thanks go to Agustín Almodóvar for his insightful conversations about the Spanish film industry, and to Lola García and Paz Sufrategui for their unwavering support. Margarita Lobo and Javier Herrera, dedicated professionals at the Filmoteca Española, have also provided invaluable film and bibliographical resources. The tireless defenders of film literature in Spain and founders of the Librería Ochoymedio, Jesús Robles and María Silveyro, provided encouragement as well as material help at crucial moments in this project. Special thanks go to Mikel Valladares of the Dartmouth College Library for a wealth of material on Spanish cinema. Marina Díaz-López, Joseba Gabilondo, Sanford Kempin, and Gene Bell-Villada form a circle of friends who have contributed substantively to the dialogue that forms the backstory of this book. Zinta Moskalew and Joanne Berg patiently provided invaluable help in the technical preparation of the manuscript. I want also to express my appreciation to the series editor, Jim Naremore, who first encouraged me to write this book and offered timely and productive editorial guidance, and to Joan Catapano of the University of Illinois Press, who has been a patient believer and supporter throughout.

Finally, this project never could have been realized without the intellectual and emotional support of Carol D'Lugo, a passionate cinephile and a lover of Almodóvar's cinema. Through her eyes and ears I learned to see and hear a different Almodóvar. I will always be in her debt.

I I I

The author and publisher gratefully acknowledge permission from the University of California to reprint Marsha Kinder, "Pleasure and the New Spanish Mentality: A Conversation with Pedro Almodóvar," *Film Quarterly* 41.1 (Fall 1987): 33–44, and Agustín Almodóvar and El Deseo S.A. for permission to reprint "Pedro Almodóvar Self-Interview *Bad Education*."

A note on translations: All translations from the Spanish are my own except where texts are quoted as indicated from published English translations.

Pedro Almodóvar |

Pedro Almodóvar and His Cinema |

Low-Level Melodrama

"Really, my story is almost a low-level melodrama," Pedro Almodóvar explains to an American interviewer. Spain's most prominent and commercially successful filmmaker, the most acclaimed European director in a generation, goes on to describe how his life, or at least the autobiography he constructs for interviewers, follows a number of patterns of melodrama, the movie genre that has been most closely identified with his own style of artistic expression:

> I mean, a boy who comes from a village just trying to survive and all these kinds of things that happen only in the movies. It's an impossible story, but it happened like that. It's a surprise that I'm making movies, because in my case it was almost impossible to dream of that. I was not born in the right place in the right family in the right town in the right language or in the right moment to make movies. But I did, so it's like dreaming of being a bullfighter when you're born in Japan or England. . . . I

wanted to be a storyteller; I just wanted to tell stories with images in movement, Super 8, 35mm, whatever. And I started doing it when I could. Before making features, I made ten years of Super 8 movies just with one small camera. For me, *that* was to be a director, not to go and be nominated for an Oscar in Hollywood. (Noh 124–25)

Almodóvar's self-description is, not surprisingly, both astute and hyperself-conscious. He has been cultivating this genre for over twenty years, reinventing his creative and biographical persona to coincide with his evolving film style. Three essential features of the evolution of his career can be discerned in his comments: his geocultural positioning, his self-invention as a film author, and his vocation as a storyteller. Let us look more closely at these.

Almodóvar's geocultural positioning is reflected in the narrative of his symbolic journey from the periphery to the center of Spanish culture, eventually leading him to occupy the improbable position of representing not only Spanish cinema but Spain itself to the outside world. Before *Women on the Verge of a Nervous Breakdown*, his films were largely conceived around aspects of local Madrid culture during the decade of Spain's transition to democracy. His style has gradually evolved to the point that when we speak of "a film by Almodóvar," though it is rooted in a specific Spanish cultural reality, it is also designed to circulate internationally. At the same time, his films conspicuously absorb certain elements of Hollywood and European cinema, most notably in the genres of film noir, melodrama, and Italian neorealism. That double movement—the passage of his films beyond the borders of Spain to international movie audiences through the absorption of an international style, and the filmmaker's self-conscious migration from social and cultural margins to the mainstream—is implied by the notion of geocultural positioning.

In the 1980s Almodóvar boasted that he made films as though Franco had never existed. As a child of traditionalist rural culture in a country run by a reactionary dictatorship, however, he was an heir to the repressive culture of the regime and the centuries-old Spanish culture of the Counter-Reformation from which Francoism drew much of its anachronistic ideology. The Spain of his formative years was a land that, decades earlier, had receded from the processes of social and artistic modernity. The spirit of Francoism was keenly felt in the rural world that shaped his early consciousness.

Almodóvar was intuitively drawn to movies at an early age. Film was treated at the time as a low form of popular entertainment, not much better than bullfights in its catering to popular tastes. In the class-bound mentality of some Spaniards, cinema was "cutre": vulgar, base, for the masses. As he tells us in his press-book commentary on *Bad Education* (2004), movie houses are "good shelter for killers and lonely people" (*La mala educacíon*). In his loneliness, movie theaters figured as prominently as movies themselves. The world that opened up on the movie screen struck a sharp contrast to the world around him. One of the legacies of the dictatorship was the cultivation of "the cult of the folkloric" that "magnified the parodic, kitsch, and sentimental in the products of mass commercial 'low' culture, primarily in the form of popular songs, religion, and bullfight culture" (Graham 239–40). Perhaps most of all, Almodóvar retained the sounds of this folkloric culture. In *What Have I Done to Deserve This?* (1985), Chus Lampreave hears the voice of Miguel de Molina, a popular-music superstar in the 1940s, singing a ballad, "La bien pagá," and pines: "How beautiful were the songs in my day." For Almodóvar, that folkloric ethos would come to mean not only nostalgia but also the persistence of a culture of anachronism. Music would eventually become the cinematic-narrative source of the acoustic imagination of characters in his films as they recall the traumatic world of their childhood.

Almodóvar's growing awareness of Spain's place in the world as a poor, backward nation came from literature, the movies, and popular music. It certainly made him attentive to a range of cultural possibilities beyond the *patria chica*, one's narrow community, and even national borders. As a child in the 1950s he became addicted to serialized soap operas on Spanish radio (Boquerini 14), a genre in which the listener's aural imagination played an integral role in filling out the melodramatic narrative. He claims that part of his effort to make sense of the world around him derived from the contrast between this provincial, folkloric culture and the movies he began to see around the age of nine in Cáceres, the regional capital. Among the most memorable were the French New Wave and Hollywood films, which must have given him the intuition that Spain was somehow inferior even in the realm of popular culture. The impact of these early experiences with foreign movies would stay with him and guide the process of his geocultural positioning.

Like other Spanish artists who, by the end of the 1960s, had become acutely aware of where they had come from and longed for something beyond, Almodóvar observed Spain's backwardness in what he read and saw. His generation experienced firsthand the contradictory transition from isolated, post–Civil War Spain to the government-orchestrated economic modernization plan that inevitably brought with it cultural modernization. It was common in those years for people to distinguish between Spain and Europe. The growing awareness of Europe, from which Spain had been spiritually disconnected by Franco and Franco-ism, would be one of the engines driving social, intellectual, and artistic change in the hinterlands.

Almodóvar came to adulthood in a Spain that, over recent decades, had witnessed intensifying internal migrations from the poorer rural regions of Galicia, Extremadura, and Andalucía to the industrial areas of Catalonia and the Basque Country and cities such as Madrid. Between 1955 and 1975, one-fifth of all Spaniards moved from the provinces to urban centers in search of economic prosperity (Riquer i Permanyer 263). By the 1960s, this migration also took the form of Spanish "guest workers" as manual laborers in Germany and as domestic workers in France. The personal migrations that characterize Almodóvar's career—from Extremadura to Cáceres to Madrid, and from a marginal figure within a marginal film culture to international prominence—mirror a chain of broader cultural migrations of Spanish society and culture. The clichéd equation between Almodóvar and Spain or Almodóvar and Spanish cinema, made by many foreign commentators, is valid, since his biography dramatizes on the individual level the metaphorical migration of Spanish culture toward integration into modern European culture, social practices, and even politics.

In an ironic way, Almodóvar's geocultural marginality was a decisive factor in his defiant belief in his potential as a filmmaker and his even-tual insistence on inventing himself as a film auteur around popular as opposed to elite culture. Early in his career, having just completed his second feature film, *Labyrinth of Passions* (1982), Almodóvar was asked by the Spanish journalist Maruja Torres what nourishes his imagination to write such complex and provocative scripts. Tellingly, he answered by defining himself and his work in contrast to the quasi-official mainstream Spanish film traditions of "cinema of quality," films based on literary adaptations of classic or contemporary novels:

> The sources that have shaped me are popular ones. You know the amount of nonsense, of imagination, that is found in the lives of those people who appear in those widely published celebrity magazines—photo novels, radio, theater, women's advice columns—the people who all of a sudden ask what they have to do to firm up their muscles or cure asthma. My sister had a fashion design shop in Extremadura, and that world stayed with me, the world of the housewife, which both delights and horrifies me at the same time because its alienation is hideous. (Torres 14)

Rooted in folkloric tradition, popular culture was not simply a prop in Almodóvar's films; he actively cultivated the blending of native and international influences as part of his evolving identity as a celebrity auteur and defender of camp (Yarza 27–28) and kitsch (Llauradó 11). In his self-conscious effort to develop a genuine artistic personality for his films, Almodóvar frequently looked to his popular roots for inspiration. By 1986, with the release of his fifth feature film, *Matador,* his cinema was already widely identified with various clichés of Andalusian folklore that had long been the hallmark of Francoist kitsch culture, including old songs and the imagery related to Catholic ritual, gypsy culture, and bullfighting (Yarza 16). As has often been noted, Almodóvar's embrace of popular culture was not a frivolous identification with these nostalgic elements but part of an aesthetic process of recycling the "desecho histórico," the historical dregs of cultural forms and styles identified with Francoist culture that his films endow with countercultural meanings (Yarza 17).

His appropriation of these elements as part of his signature style did align his films with the emergent Spanish gay culture of the post-Franco decade, particularly with his focus on drag queens and homosexuality. Alberto Mira notes, however, how Almodóvar "often defiantly expressed his unwillingness to discuss homosexuality and even gay politics, and [wouldn't] acknowledge that some elements of his work (such as camp, taste for melodrama and retro pop, use of drag queens, religious imagery, etc.) are part of 'gay culture'" (Mira, "Laws" 250). Though the culturally specific *cultura de la pluma* (Spanish gay culture) is at the heart of the artistic sensibility informing Almodóvar's films, ironically it was not until his sustained international successes in the early 1990s, when the features of Spanish camp begin to diminish in his work, that the question of his films as "gay cinema" became an issue with some commentators (Leavitt 40; Pally 32–34; Smith, *Laws* 165–68). In an interview for an extensive cover story in the *New York Times Magazine* preceding the U.S. premiere of *Bad Education,* he explains his resistance to the label:

> Even my movies that are dominated by gay characters like *Bad Education* are not meant to have a homosexual sensibility. . . . I make movies about strong passions. How a character jumps into a world to give sense to their life. I don't like to classify movies in a sexual way. To me, it's like saying, That's a fat movie by Orson Welles. Or a brunette movie by Sofia Coppola. While it's true that there is a gay culture that I draw from, this is only one influence on my films. I am not a gay director who does gay movies for a gay audience. That would not interest me. (qtd. in Hirschberg 27)

Such protestations notwithstanding, by the early 1990s Almodóvar was well established in international film circles as an openly gay filmmaker. More relevant than his biography, however, was the fact that prominent American and British scholars of his cinema (such as Marsha Kinder and Paul Julian Smith) were detailing the ways in which the melodramatic sensibility in his films did not merely repeat the formulas of Hollywood tearjerkers as camp but actually "queered" melodrama "by bringing sexual minorities to the forefront of the drama" (Williams 274). The issue of gayness as it relates to his cinema needs to be viewed within the broader context of the geocultural circulation of a discourse that is specific to a local cultural context (Spanish gay culture as an intervention in the process of social demarginalization in the decade following Franco's death) as well as to a series of transnational themes, modulated through the subversive qualities of melodrama as an expressive mode. When he describes his life as a low-level melodrama, he acknowledges his own engagement with that transnational discourse.

During the first decade of his commercial career, Almodóvar consciously cultivated the image of a celebrity auteur. His strategy was to construct what amounted to a media image of the filmmaker as celebrity through his performance art, writings, and cameo appearances in his films. He teased his audience and the critics with suggestive parallels between himself and his characters and then denied the correspondence. When asked about the parallels between his biography and his films, Almodóvar would paraphrase the Madrid journalist Francisco Umbral: "'Everything that isn't autobiographical is plagiarism'" (qtd. in Hirschberg 43). In an endless chain of newspaper and magazine interviews, television appearances, and gala premieres of his films, he developed into a media presence in Spain and orchestrated the dissolution of the lines that separate the films from the filmmaker.

The roots of Almodóvar's personal version of authorship appear to derive from one of his international models: Andy Warhol. In the early 1980s Madrid youth culture, Almodóvar was dubbed the Spanish Warhol. When Warhol visited Madrid, he met the filmmaker in an incident recalled in the introduction to Almodóvar's collection of short fiction pieces, *Patty Diphusa*. Warhol was not impressed by the suggestion of a similarity, since they didn't look much alike. "It must be because in my films I also pull out drag queens and drug addicts," he answered nervously (9). The Warhol connection was, of course, based neither on physical resemblance nor parallels between their films. It reflects the ways in which Almodóvar, like Warhol, was seen as a multitalented entrepreneur of a new cultural paradigm: writer, performer, filmmaker, actor, and authenticator of a countercultural style—in short, the celebrity author.

The Warhol association is significant, as it points up two related features of Almodóvar's early self-construction as a popular film auteur: his sense of the author as a commercial commodity, and the cultivation of an oppositional style of pop authorship that was the antithesis of Spanish art-film auteurism of the 1970s. Rather than emulating contemporary high-culture cinema, embodied in films such as Víctor Erice's *Spirit of the Beehive* (1973) or Carlos Saura's *Cría!* (1976) and *Elisa, My Life* (1977), Almodóvar's early films take a perverse pleasure in flaunting their inspiration from comic books, popular music, scatological humor, and loud colors.

As Timothy Corrigan notes of the process of film-auteur formation in the post-Vietnam era, "the auteur [becomes] a *commercial* strategy for organizing audience reception, as a critical concept bound to distribution and marketing aims that identify and address the potential cult status of an auteur" (103). In this light, we may read the Warholian revolution in cinematic aesthetics as a form of commerce transformed into art that, in its low-budget, anti-art aesthetic, is close to Almodóvar's early low-budget films (Vilarós 182). In the absence of other external forms of financial support, the entrepreneurial, self-promotional sense of the auteur was a convenient commercial as well as aesthetic approach for Almodóvar to embrace. The film auteur, a personality supported by the commercial promotion of a series of films, was in this way transformed into a celebrity.

Although filmmaking would ultimately become his overriding passion, during the early Madrid years Almodóvar was involved in theater and fictional writing as well. He performed with Fanny MacNamara, wrote *fotonovelas*, and wrote a soft-core porn novel, *Fuego en las entrañas* (Fire in the Gut; 1982), as well as a collection of first-person narratives, published in *La Luna de Madrid* under the nom de plume Patty Diphusa. He also performed in theatrical works, including an adaptation of Jean-Paul Sartre's *The Dirty Hands*, where he first met Carmen Maura, with whom his cinema would soon be closely identified.

In 1983, when his third feature film, *Dark Habits*, was shown at the Venice and Miami Film Festivals, Almodóvar found himself involuntarily representing Spain and Spanish cinema. It was an ironic position for him, since at home the industry ignored him, and establishment critics mocked his films as amateurish. Spanish filmmakers before him had been similarly treated because of their foreign successes, but Almodóvar is a distinct case since, at a time when much of Spanish cinema was unable to find foreign markets, he personified the possibility of that access abroad. Almodóvar's status as a "cinematic phenomenon," as he has often been called, thus raises the question of the nature of national cinema in Spain. Núria Triana-Toribio considers the struggle to define national cinema in Spain as a series of ideological inclusions and exclusions carried out by governmental institutions, the film industry, and the Spanish critical establishment. She cogently argues that, in the case of the marginalization of Almodóvar's cinema in Spain, the roots of the problem lie precisely in the nature of his appropriation of the popular vein in his films ("Punk" 140). His objective, as she sees it, was to connect with the broad mass of the moviegoing audience, as opposed to Spanish film auteurs of the 1970s and 1980s, who garnered only a narrow elite audience defined by class.

Although clearly the strongest defining feature of Almodóvar's cinematic signature, the multiple expressions of mass culture proved to be the most problematic for Spanish film critics during the 1980s. His musical tastes (from punk to Mexican *boleros* and Spanish *tonadillas*), his embrace of socially marginal figures (gays, drag queens, and drug addicts), and an insistence on identifying with a particular kind of popular cinema as the sources of his film citations (Spanish black comedies of the 1950s and early 1960s mixed with an improbable dose of American melodrama and screwball comedies) were cited by many Spanish reviewers as evidence of his lack of professional discipline. Spanish film scholars regularly attacked Almodóvar's films for what they viewed as shallow character development, his exploitation of the trendy style of postmodern pastiche, and an insistence on gags in place of plot development (Sánchez-Biosca).

The persistent failure of most Spanish commentators to appreciate the eccentricity of Almodóvar's storytelling strategies is, in essence, a refusal to see in his films the unique phenomenon of a popular cinematic storyteller whose style is a composite of various strains that is also, ironically, highly original. In their directness, Almodóvar's films seem antithetical to the patterns of Spanish film production that had been lionized since the early 1970s as auteur cinema and *the* national cinema. Characteristically, directors like Erice, Saura, Jaime Chávarri, and Manuel Gutiérrez Aragón had constructed characters traumatized by their national history. By contrast, Almodóvar's early characters' motivations are simple, uncomplicated, and nearly always rooted in the here and now. As complex as his plots may be, the motivations of his characters are always transparent. As he often says, these derive from the model of popular Hollywood cinema of the 1940s and 1950s, popular magazines, television programs, and popular music. He found the formal sources for the narrative style of *Pepi, Luci, Bom, and Other Girls on the Heap* (1980) in comic books and the popular magazines of the day.

In *Dark Habits* (1983), Sister Rat is inspired to write lurid best sellers from the stories of the fallen women who have come to the convent of the Humbled Redeemers. Desire and passion are at the root of Almodóvar's narrative energy.

There is a quintessential moment in *Women on the Verge of a Nervous Breakdown* (1988) when Pepa (Carmen Maura) pursues her former lover to his apartment building. In a parody of Hitchcock's *Rear Window*, she stands outside peering into the various windows, as if enchanted by the stories unfolding before her eyes. As one astute critic notes, Pepa quickly moves out of her self-absorbed world and becomes interested in what she sees, in effect "transferring sexual desire into a desire for narrative" (Deleyto 54). This moment reveals one of the central components of Almodóvar's cinema: the desire for and delirious enjoyment of stories. It may be in response to that desire for story and its twin, the delight in narrating, that Almodóvar has developed such a prodigious array of embedded digressions in his films that so often seem on the verge of collapsing into narrative chaos, but never do.

In his notes on *Talk to Her* (2002), he writes: "Disrupted time and the mixing of diverse narrative units function best when the action is mental or internal, or occurs in another dimension, as in the films of David Lynch. In this kind of 'fantastic neorealism' or 'naturalism of the absurd' in which I move, plot ruptures suppose a kind of punch in the eyes of the spectator since he's already bonded with the characters and the story, and I pull him away, grab him, and oblige him to follow another character, another story." Rather than diminishing the desire for story, these "punches in the eye" intensify viewers' delight with the storytelling process.

Such techniques suggest that, as a consummate, if unconventional, storyteller, Almodóvar is always aware that there is a purpose to the story and the narrative act, even as it is embedded in popular culture clichés. This may be why there is a characteristic and insistent recontextualizing process involved in every one of his narratives. In *Kika*, for example, Nicolás Pierce, a serial killer, is also a novelist who recycles his bloody murders into the plots of his misogynistic best sellers.

Through cinematic self-reference, particularly the device of the film-within-the-film and related forms of movie quotations, Almodóvar's plots move across social and geographic barriers, "plundering the spoils of foreign lands," as Michel de Certeau describes the activity of the textual poacher (174), aligning new meanings with old stories. If Almodóvar's cinematic stories are both legible and appealing to international audiences, it is not simply the inexplicable genius of the filmmaker but the talent of the eclectic craftsman who knows how to develop stories as collages that produce the ironic and multiple readings that appeal to a broad range of spectators. At their core, however, his stories are rooted in an effort to use narrative to provide a logic to actions and lives, to dramatize the identity of characters that occupy the emotional center of Almodóvar's films.

At what may be the pivotal moment in *Talk to Her,* Benigno, the nurse, describes to the comatose dancer, Alicia, the plot of a silent movie he has just seen, *The Shrinking Lover.* The story he tells, which Almodóvar portrays in one of his most brilliant constructions of a film-within-a-film, is only retrospectively understood as a curtain to mask Benigno's rape of Alicia. But it has another purpose, as well. Both the story and the act of storytelling reflect Benigno's effort to transform himself from a predatory rapist into a sympathetic figure. Storytelling serves as a performative act in Almodóvar's films, self-consciously providing explanatory coherence to characters as well as to their audience. In telling the story of an impossible love, Benigno is really constructing a new identity for himself.

In the long evolution of Almodóvar's cinematic style, the desire for story has remained constant. As suggested by the celebrity author's teasing of his interviewers, the most tantalizing of all his stories is his own. There is no "official" biography of Pedro Almodóvar, although the pressbooks that accompany his films include an increasingly detailed profile of the dates and facts of his life. At crucial junctures of his career he has offered personal observations, either to explain the presence of a theme or to disclaim any literal autobiographical links, as was the case with *Law of Desire* (1987) and *Bad Education* (2004), which feature gay filmmakers as protagonists. Speaking of Francoism with clear autobiographical implications, Almodóvar commented: "We don't have confidence in the future, but we are constructing a past for ourselves because we don't like the one we have" (Kinder, "Pleasure" 37). These are the details as he has "invented" them:

Though some sources list 1951 as the year of his birth, Pedro Almodóvar was born on September 25, 1949, in the rural town of Calzada de la Calatrava in the Manchegan province of Ciudad Real. The region of his birth and formative years represents the social milieu that would be the setting for some of Spanish cinema's harshest depictions of rural life of this period—films like Luis García Berlanga's comic but bitter attack on the backwardness of rural underdevelopment by the Franco regime, *Bienvenido Mister Marshall* (Welcome Mister Marshall; 1952), Juan Antonio Bardem's *Calle Mayor* (Main Street; 1956), and Fernando Fernán-Gómez's *El extraño viaje* (The Strange Journey; 1963). There is a common refrain among Spanish film critics who assume a simple correlation between Almodóvar's roots in rural Spain during the second decade of the dictatorship and his later cinematic sensibilities: "The situation the country lived through during the years of his childhood would determine his way of making films and viewing life" (Colmenero Salgado 17). María Antonia García de León and Teresa Maldenado argue that the insistent identification of Almodóvar's origins in La Mancha is intended to emphasize an environment of poverty, social backwardness, economic underdevelopment, and forced migration to other parts of Spain (30). His Manchegan roots would make him something of an outsider among filmmakers who, by and large, were of comfortable middle-class backgrounds with the benefits of an urban cultural formation.

Almodóvar would claim to have only faint memories of his early years in the Manchegan village: "I recall my sisters and my mother talking in the patios with the neighbors and sewing. . . . It was very García Lorca, very folkloric. And, as a small child, going with my mother to a well that was there in the fields where all the women of the district would get together to wash clothes in the open air, and stuff like that" (Alabadejo et al. 36). In a characteristic attempt to fend off psychological readings of his life, he observes: "My childhood was not sad, nor was it happy. The looks that I got from my early childhood were disapproving. I didn't know what they were disapproving, because I was only a little kid, but the judgment was already made. I don't want to dramatize the case, but it was hard. By luck, it didn't traumatize me because I have a very optimistic personality and because I took refuge in reading and movies, which gave me enormous pleasure" (Strauss, *Conversaciones* 18).

In one of the earliest serious interviews in which the theme of his gay sensibility is nonchalantly posed, Almodóvar further details his childhood: "I wasn't a normal child, and fortunately that didn't traumatize me. I liked to read, which seemed odd. During recess I'd rather talk about Ava Gardner, for example, because even though I didn't know all that well who she was, I knew that she had had fifteen husbands, and that amused me more than playing" (Harguindey 34).

Years later, the Spanish writer Vicente Verdú included Almodóvar as a prominent member of a generation of "Spaniards without complexes," artists unlike those who had come to prominence in the 1960s and 1970s. That earlier generation's quest for artistic identity grew out of their awareness of Spain's marginalization within Europe. Many of them turned the theme of Spain as problem into the essence of their writings (Juan Goytisolo in the novel, Antonio Buero Vallejo in the theater, and, most famously, Carlos Saura and Víctor Erice in cinema).

Almodóvar spent his early years in Calzada de la Calatrava, one of four children (two boys, two girls). His family's social position could be called modest, related to agriculture. His father, Antonio Almodóvar, who could barely read or write (Mackenzie 154), worked most of his life as a muleteer, one of the last in Spain, hauling barrels of wine by mule (García de León and Maldonado 26). Almodóvar's mother, Francisca Caballero, turned him into a part-time teacher of literacy in the village and also a letter reader and transcriber for the neighbors. Hoping that the eight-year-old Pedro might someday become a priest, the family sent him to study at a religious boarding school in the nearby city of Cáceres, the Colegio de los Salesianos. Almodóvar recalls the shock of moving from the village to a city: "'For me, Cáceres in the sixties was like Paris in the seventies'" (qtd. in Boquerini 14). In Cáceres, the young Pedro first became fascinated with popular cinema from Spain and Hollywood.

He would later recall that down the street from the religious school was the theater where he saw many of the films that his spiritual director was certain would lead him to hell: "Frank Tashlin or Blake Edwards, some by Billy Wilder. *Two for the Road* (1967) by Stanley Donen, which I liked a lot. In Cáceres, we also saw the first French New Wave films, *The Four Hundred Blows*, . . . the great Italian neorealist films, the first films by Pasolini, Visconti, and those by Antonioni which I always remember because they moved me so much. None of them spoke about my life but, curiously, I felt very close to the world they revealed to me. When I saw *L'Avventura* (1960), I felt very shaken up, and I said to myself, 'My

God, this picture is talking about me'" (Strauss, *Conversaciones* 14). His comment about the impact of *L'Avventura,* like the movie citations in his films, says much about the sense of entrapment and isolation Almodóvar must have experienced during his adolescence: "'Cinema became my real education,'" he would tell interviewers, "'much more than the one I received from the priests'" (qtd. in Hirschberg 40).

The family eventually joined him in Cáceres, where his father opened a gas station, and his mother, staying faithful to her village roots, established a *bodega* where she sold her own wine. Pedro parodied his experiences in Calzada de la Calatrava and Cáceres in an essay, "Advice on How to Become an Internationally Famous Director" (reprinted in *Patty Diphusa*). His first advice was to get on the next bus to Madrid (*Patty* 195). To one of the many interviewers who asked about his childhood in Extremadura, he responded: "All I ever dreamed about was getting out of there. I knew that somewhere there was a place for me" (Mackenzie 161). He finally managed to do exactly that. Against his parents' wishes, he moved to Madrid in 1967 at the age of seventeen: "I came to Madrid, and then, just as I arrived, there were, socially and literally speaking, two great explosions: one was the last cry of the hippy movement, and the other was the boom of South American literature. As soon as I arrived, I read in a newspaper that there was this boom, and I said to myself, 'I'm going to see what it's all about'" (Alabadejo 37).

Almodóvar witnessed a Madrid that had already begun to break from the conservativism of the Old Spain. His experience mirrors in microcosm the post-Franco transition that began to take shape during the final eight years of the dictatorship. Within a year, Almodóvar had transformed himself, somewhat schizophrenically, from a provincial into "someone modern" (Alabadejo 37). He was a phone-company functionary by day who morphed into a hippy and alternative-culture performer by night.

The final years of the Franco dictatorship witnessed the ebullience of the approaching freedom of expression and the last efforts of the repressive regime to contain dissidence. The 1970 *ley de peligrosidad social* (social deviance law) gave police the power to arrest people who appeared to be homosexual, viewing them as a social threat. Reflecting on that aspect of his youth in Madrid, Almodóvar later commented: "It was not a good time to have a sexual orientation that was different. . . . There were some homosexual experiences in the village when I was about thirteen, fourteen, but these were with bisexuals, so I don't think I knew then, I think I accepted it when I was eighteen. In Madrid I was always able to live in a natural way. I was lucky" (Mackenzie 159).

Those early years in Madrid enabled Almodóvar to view films at the Filmoteca, while devouring an eclectic range of literature. The National Film School had been branded by the government as a hotbed of communists and was summarily closed in 1970. Given his precarious economic circumstances, there was no way for him to learn filmmaking except by his own dogged determination. His early fascination with movies took on a more active form: He worked as an extra in a few commercial films and started to shoot Super 8 shorts: "What I had clear in my mind was that I wanted to tell stories with images. A Super 8 camera fell into my hands, and that was it: images! It was all the same to me that there was no sound, that the storyline made no sense, because from my perspective, Super 8 represented cinema. It was cheap, and you had the freedom to do whatever you wanted" (Boyero 43–44). He began showing some of his Super 8 shorts at parties and short-film festivals in Barcelona, the center of underground film culture and sexual freedom at the time. In Barcelona he fell in with a group of alternative artists who were considered the vanguard by the norms of the day. But Almodóvar's determined emphasis on narrative films quickly set him apart. He continued showing his shorts in Madrid and Barcelona, becoming known in both cities as a Super 8 filmmaker.

The series of Super 8 shorts that he began showing in 1974 included such titles as *Dos putas o historias de amor que termina en boda* (Two Whores, or Stories of Love That End with Marriage; 1974), *Film político* (A Political Film; 1974), *Blancor* (1975), *Salomé* (16mm, 1976), *Muerte en la carretera* (Death on the Highway; 35 mm, 1976), *Sexo va, sexo viene* (Sex Comes, Sex Goes; 1977), and "*Folle . . . Folle . . . Fólleme, Tim* (Fuck . . . Fuck . . . Fuck Me, Tim; 1978, with Carmen Maura). The scandalous title of the last of these puns on the Spanish word *folletín*, a serialized radio melodrama. Technically, *Folle . . . Tim* was a feature-length film, running ninety minutes; it was shot in Super 8. All of these films were satirical in spirit, parodying established genres. Since there were no commercial venues for screening Super 8 films, Almodóvar's works were often shown in Madrid at friends' apartments or, on rare occasions, at the Filmoteca or the university's communication school.

Since there were no soundtracks for any of his films, not even *Folle . . . Tim*, Almodóvar had to improvise sound, dialogue, and commentary for his screenings: "I myself in person accompanied the projection, with kinds of commentaries and dubbing the voices of all the actors. Everything was direct. 'Direct Sound' is what I called what came out of my mouth and went directly to the ears of the spectators. My brother Agustín used to help me with the music; when I signaled to him, he'd put on a cassette with background music we had chosen earlier. The screenings turned into authentic parties. A 'happening' is what they called it in those days" (Strauss, *Conversaciones* 20).

This image of Pedro Almodóvar speaking over the projected images recalls the earliest experience of Luis Buñuel at public screenings of *Un Chien Andalou*. Almodóvar's conception was not, however, rooted in silent film. Even at this early stage of his apprenticeship, the awareness of soundtrack forms a meaningful link with Buñuel. For each, the dynamic juxtaposition of sound to image was not to secure the verisimilitude of the image but for more complex and subversive reasons.

Of the shorts that Almodóvar made during this period, the most significant was *Salomé*, the only one shot in 16mm. This was his first time working with professional actors using 16mm equipment, the format in which he would shoot his first feature-length film. *Salomé* represents a crucial bridge in Almodóvar's career (Boquerini 28). He said of *Folle . . . Tim*, "My only ambition was to tell a story and have audiences understand it" (Strauss, *Conversaciones* 20). Another chance to tell his story would arise shortly with *Pepi, Luci, Bom, and Other Girls on the Heap*.

Pepi, Luci, Bom, and Other Friends of Pedro

Almodóvar's first two commercial features, *Pepi, Luci, Bom, y otra chicas del montón* (Pepi, Luci, Bom, and Other Girls on the Heap; 1980) and *Laberinto de pasiones* (Labyrinth of Passions; 1982), have often been characterized as chronicles of Madrid's youth culture in the years immediately following Franco's death and the beginning of the political transition to democracy (Mazierska and Rascaroli 30–31). More closely rooted in contemporary social history and creativity than most of his subsequent filmmaking, these works present an urban milieu that embodies the geocultural repositioning of Spain within modernity through the motif of physical movement (*movida*) and the prodigious force of a new narrative centered in pop culture. Almodóvar's self-promotional authorship is made apparent through his onscreen appearances with drag queens, masochistic wives, nymphomaniacs, rock performers, and others. As author-in-the-text, he metaphorically embodies new cultural identities emerging from previously marginalized groups. Weaving together national and foreign cultural elements, the antic plots Almodóvar devises in these early works narrate variations of a common post-Franco story of a generational rupture that entails the unshackling of Spaniards from the constraints of the recent past and the assertion of a direct connection to international culture (Valis 280–82). Together, the films constitute an ongoing parody of social and storytelling conventions filtered through the young director's "voluntad de estilo," a willful desire to construct his own unique filmmaking style (Zunzunegui 177).

We see the geocultural dimension in *Pepi, Luci, Bom*'s celebration of Madrid as the site of a generational break from Spain's past, where youthful characters seek to identify with international youth culture, principally through popular music (Allinson, "Construction" 268). The analogous joke that underlies *Labyrinth of Passions* is that "Madrid is the most entertaining city in the world." *Labyrinth*'s plot combines a fairy-tale narrative (the prince who finally reencounters his true love) with topical news related to the exiled Shah of Iran to produce a story that embraces hybrid forms of expression and experience. As Ewa Mazierska and Laura Rascaroli argue, these early films depict a utopian, asocial Madrid, highly inflected by the filmmaker's deeply personal style and yet "realistically symptomatic of present problems and lifestyles" (31).

The source of creative inspiration for characters in both films lies in their relation to the international punk culture of the 1970s. As Núria Triana-Toribio comments on Almodóvar's absorption of the style: "Almodóvar [is] one of those urban youths absorbing punk as it came from the USA and Europe and supplementing it with autocthonous elements within that creative atmosphere" ("Punk" 274). The Spanish expression of that transnational cultural mix is located in the youth-culture movement of the late 1970s and early 1980s, what has been called *La movida madrileña*. The term is either "a slanguish pun on the Francoist *Movimiento*" (Triana-Toribio, "Punk" 275) or a reference to drug use: *hacerse una movida,* according to Javier Escudero, meant to buy drugs (148). Both derivations irreverently express a generational break from conservative Francoist culture.

Almodóvar's relation to *La movida* is rooted foremost in his collaboration with Fabio de Miguel, a.k.a. Fanny MacNamara, in the musical group Almodóvar y MacNamara, whose performance strategies "relied heavily on those of 1960s New York Pop style" of figures associated with Andy Warhol (Triana-Toribio, "Punk" 277). Almodóvar appears in *Labyrinth of Passion* in partial drag, singing "Suck It to Me" in English. This international punk linkage had earlier been established in *Pepi, Luci, Bom,* in which an English-language punk song accompanies the opening credits. One of the three protagonists, Bom, is played by the punk singer Olvido Gara, a.k.a. Alaska, accompanied in musical numbers by her band, Los Pegamoides, renamed Los Bomitoni after her role in the film.

The artists of *La movida* adopted a position often described as *pasotismo* (indifference or lethargy, even a defiant apoliticism), which, Almodóvar would argue, was itself a political position that rejected the *progres,* those who had come to political power during the Transition (Vernon and Morris 11). He says of the spirit of the period and its rejection of a political posture: "'There existed a very independent playfulness. You did things because it was fun to do them. In a certain respect, frivolity became a political position in order to pose a way of life that absolutely rejected boredom. The apoliticism of those years was a very healthy response to all the disastrous political activity that had achieved nothing'" (qtd. in Gallero 219).

In his earliest screen cameos in *Pepi, Luci, Bom* and two sketches in which he appears with MacNamara in *Labyrinth of Passions,* Almodóvar is identified as a performer-personality, and his performances demonstrate opposition to the bourgeois mores of Spanish society: In the Erecciones Generales sequence in *Pepi* he mocks politics and defies good taste and heterosexual culture. In the "Suck It to Me" number in *Labyrinth* he imitates English, foreign, and gay-figured musical performers. Read in the context of his subsequent development, these early appearances suggest the precocious forging of an authorial identity that privileges performance as one of the marks of identity, breaking down the traditional borders between public and private.

Paul Julian Smith has proposed that Almodóvar's meteoric rise to international prominence is in part the result of "the support of the gay press and gay audiences" (*Laws* 165). He argues that these early films reflect the crossover between the art and fashion worlds, aligning the gay scene in Madrid with Warhol's New York of the previous decade (167). According to Smith, the film's international appeal derives from its partaking of the Warholesque interest in characters who are the epitome of the underground: male prostitutes and drag queens (176).

The aesthetic formula of *Pepi, Luci, Bom* is to be found in the series of incongruous juxtapositions between national and foreign cultures. At a rock concert, Kiti Manver explains to her friends that Flamenco Rock "is like a *tonadilla* [a traditional Andalusian ballad], but only a little bit more international in flavor" (Yarza 40). In his review of *Pepi, Luci, Bom* in *El País,* Diego Galán praises the multiple recyclings of those elements of pop culture that constitute the film's distinctive quality. The title of his review captures that sense: "Con Groucho Marx y Mae West." The question for Galán is not the originality or even the competence of the work; he recognizes that these are at times notably lacking. Rather, it is the affirmation of a popular culture that renders its audience complicit in its attacks on the culture of good taste. It also embodies a gay camp sensibility clearly linked to the Warhol aesthetic, what Alejandro Yarza calls the recycling of the dregs of cultural production (23). Partly in jest, Almodóvar characterizes his use of diverse cultural elements in his films of this period as not only plagiarism but also outright theft: "The more we plagiarized, the more authentic we were" (Almodóvar, *Patty* 8). Such an aesthetic emulates the international style of Warholesque pop/camp (Yarza 46), as it diminishes the impact of Spanish culture. Yet, at its root, such an aesthetic is not a mere aping of foreign sources but an effort to Hispanicize them, constructing a Spanish modernity founded on the principle of cultural hybridity.

The origin of *Pepi, Luci, Bom* dates to the period in which Almodóvar had already completed the feature-length Super 8 film *Folle . . . Folle . . . Folléme, Tim* and was involved with the independent theater company Los Goliardos, while also writing punk comics for the alternative magazine *Star.* One punk comic project was entitled *Erecciones generales* (General Erections), a wordplay on the 1977 Spanish general elections. At the time, Almodóvar had a small part in a play in which Carmen Maura was one of the leads. In her dressing room he would read her the plotlines he had developed for the comic. She urged him to develop *Erecciones generales* into a film script (Vidal, *El cine* 16). Agreeing to acquire the financial backing for the project and also to appear in the film, she suggested that he change the title (Strauss, *Conversaciones* 26). Almodóvar was further encouraged by Maura's fellow actor, Félix Rotaeta, and their mutual friend, the film critic Diego Galán.

Working with Rotaeta, Maura contacted hundreds of friends and acquaintances, asking them to join a production collective to back the film. Their help also brought in the services of technicians, many of whom had never worked on a film before. In a variety of interviews, Almodóvar recalled the experience of the eighteen months in 1979 and 1980 during which the filming took place. The lengthy shooting time was needed in this artesan approach to filmmaking since, as a volunteer activity, it was done largely after work and on weekends. Complicating the project was the fact that *Pepi, Luci, Bom* was being shot in 16mm. For the film to be commercially viable, it had to be blown up to a 35mm format, which required a larger budget than the group had. At one point, what looked like the completed version ran only fifty minutes, obviously not sufficient for commercial distribution. More money was needed, as well as more narrative "filler." Further backing by the Catalan producer Pepón Coromina enabled Almodóvar to shoot a sequence in a discothèque and to expand Fanny MacNamara's role, bringing the film to commercial-distribution length (Riambau 127–28).

Most Spanish critics panned *Pepi, Luci, Bom* as a substandard commercial film. Almodóvar, however, looks back fondly to the freedom in which it was developed: "*Pepi, Luci, Bom* . . . is a film full of defects. When a film has only one or two, it's considered an imperfect film, while when there's a profusion of technical flaws, it's called style. That's what I said joking around when I was promoting the film, but I believe that that was close to the truth" (Strauss, *Conversaciones* 27). *Pepi, Luci, Bom* has been read as a highly self-conscious effort by Almodóvar to forge a style from a diverse patchwork of recycled elements (Zunzunegui 171–74).

Among the film's technical flaws to which Almodóvar alludes, commentators most often mentioned the glaring problem of framing in the General Erections scene, in which Almodóvar's head was partially cut off by the upper frame when the 16mm copy was enlarged to 35mm, and the lack of continuity in the opening sequence: "In *Pepi* there are three shots, in each of which—edited to be shown one right after the other—there was a six-month difference in shooting. The hair isn't the same, the face is, well, . . . Olvido [Gara] began as a girl and ended up as a woman in the film. She started [filming] when she was fifteen, and we finished when she was seventeen. Carmen goes to answer the door to let Félix in in June of 1979, she opens it in December of '79, and the first shots of Félix and her seated together is June of '80. That scene is shot in three different times and put together one shot after another. If you look carefully, you'll see that her ponytails are different" (Alabadejo 40).

Almodóvar has described his creation of complex and detailed biographies for each of the three female protagonists (Boquerini 34–36). Though never used, they reveal a quality of depth for the characters and their backstories that is usually ignored by critics of his early work. It also suggests the prodigious nature of Almodóvar's storytelling imagination. In the early films, especially in *Labyrinth*, a rich choral effect is created by the array of characters. In his later works, however, the complexity of the stories surrounding each character eventually wins out. That subsequent development has its roots in *Pepi*. For most audiences, the seemingly disjunctive narrative elements are held together by the figure of Carmen Maura. Maura had by this point established herself as a young *progre* figure in films like Fernando Colomo's *Tigres de papel* (Paper Tigers; 1977) and *¿Qué hace una chica como tú en un sitio como éste?* (What's a Girl Like You Doing in a Place Like This?; 1978). Her embodiment of that liberal middle-class spirit would be the foil against which the figure of Pepi evolved.

Against the figure of Pepi as a link to conventional cinematic storytelling, we note a persistent effort to sabotage normative cinematic narrative logic by assaulting narrative continuity from a variety of angles. Though it is easy to read the plot of *Pepi, Luci, Bom* as a fragmented and chaotic expression of an emerging generation of alienated youth looking to foreign culture as a source of identification, the film is constructed as an affirmation of a series of "little narratives" of ruptures with the recent Spanish past and all forms of social authority. The storyline, such as it is, is presented in the style of comic *fotonovelas*. Each sequence is prefaced with a comic strip–style title provided by the graphic artist Ceesepe. The film begins with an English-language punk song and a cartoon image of the three heroines, announcing its international, distancing, and deforming perspective toward contemporary Madrid. Pepi (Maura), self-described as a wealthy heiress, remains financially dependent on her father; she lives alone in Madrid. Raped by a police inspector (Félix Rotaeta), she swears vengeance. Enlisting the help of the rock band Bomitoni in exchange for her marijuana plants, Pepi has them assault the inspector on the street, only to discover the next day that they had actually beaten up his twin brother. Undaunted, she pursues the inspector's wife, Luci (Eva Siva), whom she persuades to come to her apartment for knitting lessons. Their lesson is interrupted by the arrival of Bom (Alaska), who is immediately smitten by Luci. As a masochist, Luci responds to Bom's aggressive behavior and is in ecstasy when the teenage rocker urinates over her.

Therein follows a series of adventures that do little to advance the plot. The three women attend a block party where a contest of "General Erections" is officiated by Almodóvar. A bisexual voyeur and his bearded wife (Cristina Pascual) observe from a nearby window while having sex. Later, when her father refuses her further financial support, Pepi becomes a creative writer for advertising spots. The police inspector eventually catches up with his wife at a discothèque, where he beats her so aggressively that she must be hospitalized. When her two friends finally locate Luci at the hospital, they discover that she has reconciled with her husband, whose physical abuse is the perfect solution to her masochistic desires. The film ends as Pepi and Bom set out to find happiness on their own.

Such an emphasis on a pop form of storytelling, exemplified by the integration of the *fotonovela* format, suggests the frivolousness of forms of popular narration embraced by Almodóvar. But the presumed linearity of that form is frequently broken up by digressions that interrupt the plot, such as the vignette of the couple having sex during the General Erections sequence, the insertion of Pepi's sketch for a television commercial advertising women's panties, or even the series of preposterous coincidences, such as the introduction of the police detective's twin brother. Santos Zunzunegui argues that the juxtaposition of these incongruous elements against a seemingly simple storyline undermines the logic of dramatic causality. Yet Almodóvar has it both ways. His plot seems to adhere to the logic of a recognizable causal chain of events, yet that causality is continually interrupted by inane elements that destroy the logic of characters and action (Zunzunegui 174).

Set against the quirkiness of the film's neobaroque plotting is a group of uncomplicated characters whose actions and responses arise from immediate desire or emotion. After having viewed the brooding, introspective dramas about the traumas of the Civil War and its aftermath that garnered so much attention from Spanish film reviewers, in *Pepi* Almodóvar addressed Spanish audiences generally ignored by that kind of cinema. "The country is going through some of the most interesting moments, and what we really need is for us directors to talk about this period. . . . [T]he focus of filmmakers is in the past, in the postwar era, and these are ghosts that half the country doesn't identify with because we don't have them" (Llauradó 13). His preference for making comedies instead of the complex symbolic narratives that characterize the much-praised auteurist films of Víctor Erice, Carlos Saura, and Manuel Gutiérrez Aragón was an unmistakable reflection of Almodóvar's repudiation of the Spanish critical establishment's notion of "national" Spanish cinema (Triana-Toribio, *Spanish* 135).

Beneath that frivolous, in-your-face style, however, and especially significant in terms of the film's presumed testimonial quality as a chronicle of the *movida* years, *Pepi, Luci, Bom* invokes contemporary Spanish history. The parody of the general elections of June 1977 and the attempted coup of February 1981, presciently posed through Luci's fascistic husband, who is frequently identified with right-wing politics, frame the film's actions. Elements of Francoist culture and that of the Transition are recycled and charged with new countercultural meanings (Yarza 17), as in the scene in which the Bomitoni use the traditional *zarzuela* song to lure their victim, the detective's twin brother, into approaching them. For all the parodic treatment of the past, however, the underlying cultural logic of Almodóvar's first two films and *La movida* that shapes them is "the refusal and inability to come to terms with the past" (Valis 282).

The disjointed and digressive plot of *Pepi, Luci, Bom* that underscores the conflict between Pepi and the police detective comes to embody the political tension between the representatives of international modernity and the Francoist old guard. As Almodóvar notes, because the characters derive from a comic book rather than a cinematic source, they tend to be "obvious stereotypes, quickly recognizable and typical of the narrative form that framed them: the modern girl and the bad cop. They don't require any psychological development" (Strauss, *Conversaciones* 27). Ironically, by this extreme stereotyping, Almodóvar's script achieves a modified version of the kind of allegorical narrative that was the staple of the symbol-laden cinema he reviled (that of directors like Saura and Gutiérrez Aragón).

Playing against Spanish auteur cinema of the 1970s that was steeped in the traumas of the past, Almodóvar reduces Francoism to a series of comic anecdotes and verbal gags. As the film suggests, the real question for Spaniards is not about the past but about modernity, often tied aesthetically to questions of representation. We may read the plot as a statement of the creative positionings for the artist in that effervescent world that would soon assume the name of *La movida:* the narrative frame of comics, the foregrounding of the Bomitoni and of Alaska as singer, and Pepi's career as a creative publicity writer.

Almodóvar replaces Spain's recent political history with a self-conscious emphasis on the importance of performance as an expression of individual identity. In one pivotal sequence, Pepi proposes to film the biographies of her two friends. As she explains, "Not only do you have to be yourselves, but you have to represent yourselves as characters. Representation is always a very artificial thing." As Almodóvar explains to Nuria Vidal: "'The video [discussion] is pure theory and a lot of bull on my part. At the same time, it's a curious exercise to talk about film within a film, talking to the fictional characters. It's as if I myself got into the film and started talking not to Eva Siva but to her character, Luci, explaining to her what she should be. Sometimes, the characters have to be more in order for others to see them'" (qtd. in Vidal, *El cine* 26).

Later in the film, during Bom and the Bomitoni's concert performance, we see an additional twist on this concept of performing identity. Reworking the cliché of life inspiring art, Bom sings a love song to Luci,

"You're a pig from Murcia" (*Marrana murciana*). The mini-essay on representations combines with the "biographical" ballad to suggest that the film's patchwork of hybrid narratives is not mere frivolity but part of an effort to convey the story of newly emerging identities through a popular medium.

This attempt to construct new identities is linked throughout to a multifaceted parody of recognizable narrative forms, the aim of which is to undermine old meanings and to rewrite them into new contexts. The process of rewriting involves perhaps the most ambitious aspect of Almodóvar's scripting of *Pepi:* the onscreen "staging" of audiences to bear witness to "the deconstruction of the classical binary oppositions of masculine/feminine, high/low culture, naturalness/artifice" (Yarza 44). This is the implicit logic that guides the ambitious General Erections sequence, which actually consists of two scenes: the couple in the apartment, and the spectacle of the contest itself. The apartment scene, involving the bearded woman speaking lines that parody the words of Maggie, the Cat, from Tennessee Williams's *Cat on a Hot Tin Roof,* serves another crucial positioning function. Not only does the scene frame the action of the sexual spectacle below, but the evocation of Williams's lines further breaks the limiting Spanish context of the action by evoking an international gay playwright and a work about suppressed homosexual identity.

The distancing element functions to undo the binding of that audience to the aesthetic object. We see this perhaps most pointedly in the publicity spot interpolated into the narrative. "¡Ponte bragas!" follows the parodic style of Almodóvar's early Super 8 spoofs of television commercials, combining the bourgeois ideology of consumerism with the assault on middle-class taste (Holguín 119). In the sequence, Cecilia Roth demonstrates a new brand of absorbent panties, ¡Ponte! (literally, "Put 'em on!"), that absorbs odors and liquid and allows the wearer to urinate in public.

Pepi, Luci, Bom premiered at the 1980 San Sebastián Film Festival and was later shown to enthusiastic audiences at the Sevilla Film Festival. The film's reception clearly suggests the emergence of an audience that had not been taken into account by the dominant forces directing the Spanish film industry. Though produced for a mere six million pesetas (roughly ninety thousand dollars), the film garnered forty-three million pesetas in its initial Madrid release and remained for a three-year run at the Alphaville Theater's weekend cult midnight screenings.

Labyrinthine Passions

Almodóvar's second film was more ambitious than *Pepi, Luci, Bom*. It was produced by Musidora, the owners of the Alphaville multiplex in Madrid, and had a much more substantial budget: twenty-one million pesetas. Although still absurdly low for the period, the budget allowed for certain technical advances over *Pepi*. Almodóvar liked to jest that *Labyrinth of Passions* was a film you could both hear and see, self-derisively referring to the poor sound and lighting in *Pepi*. Despite these technical improvements and a script that showed the young director's mastery of a more conventional narrative form, the film was attacked in the Spanish press, ironically, for not being as scandalous and offensive as *Pepi*. This led Almodóvar to defend it more than any other of his early works (Vidal, *El cine* 64).

Labyrinth of Passions was more commercially successful than *Pepi*, quickly achieving cult status. It played at the Alphaville's popular weekend midnight screenings for over a year. Almodóvar considered *Labyrinth* a reworking of the Hollywood screwball comedy, a genre he identified with Billy Wilder. It appeared to owe more to the fast-talking variation of that genre of the 1930s, particularly films in the style of Preston Sturges (Strauss, *Conversaciones* 34): "'The screwball comedy is a genre I like a lot. There are always a thousand things that are happening, the characters are running without a stop, chasing one another, crossing paths, running up and down, without stopping for a moment'" (qtd. in Vidal, *El cine* 43–44). The antic humor of the plot is modulated around a more recent model, as Almodóvar acknowledges: Richard Lester's pop narrative style (*A Hard Day's Night;* 1964) provided a comedic format more in keeping with the urban milieu of *Labyrinth* (44).

Labyrinth of Passions represents the first extensive example of the devilishly complex plotting that characterizes many of Almodóvar's later commercial feature-length films. There seem to be no backstories in this narrative. All the details of the characters' identities, their past and present hang-ups, are laid out as integral to the main plot, which goes something like this: Toraya, the former Empress of Tiran (Helga Liné), visits Madrid to see her gynecologist and discovers that, at last, she is fertile. She learns that her stepson, Riza (Imanol Arias), is in Madrid and sets out to find him. In the meantime, Riza has a sexual encounter with a medical student, Sadec (Antonio Banderas), who is really a member of an Islamic fundamentalist group searching for Riza to kidnap him. When Riza discovers that Sadec is Tiranian, he flees the student's apartment and seeks help from Fabio MacNamara, who provides him with a disguise. Riza assumes the identity of a rock singer and performs in a nightclub, where he meets and falls in love with Sexilia, the daughter of his stepmother's gynecologist.

Sexilia (Cecilia Roth) introduces an extensive flashback as she explains the complicated origins of her nymphomania to her Argentine psychiatrist (Ofelia Angélica). As a child she was at the beach playing with a young boy, Riza as a child, who was carried away by his stepmother, Toraya. When Sexilia came crying to her father, he was too busy to attend to her. Rejected by her father, she gave herself to five boys on the beach. One of these, in turn, went off with Riza. The flashback thus explains the origins of the sexual hang-ups of both protagonists and establishes the pivotal point of the film's narrative resolution—the reuniting of Sexilia with Riza as a corrective for the sexual problems of each.

This already zany storyline is intersected by the story of Queti (Marta Fernández Muro), a young woman who works in her father's dry-cleaning shop. Her delusional father (Luis Ciges) imagines that Queti is really his wife, who had run off with another man, and makes love to her on alternating days. Queti strikes up a friendship with Sexilia, whom she admires, and eventually has herself made over as Sexilia's double. Together, the lookalikes are able to resolve part of Sexilia's problem with her father by having Queti-Sexilia make love with the gynecologist. In this way, the film underscores the rejection of patriarchal desire as one of the mechanisms propelling the plot, while at the same time mocking all forms of psychoanalytic solutions to the questions of desire.

Alberto Mira locates the conceptual center of the film in its gay camp project, which, among other things, poses a parodic attitude toward all scientific discourses, especially those related to sexuality (*Sodoma* 558). Thus the centrality of gay and cross-dressing characters (Imanol Arias and Antonio Banderas, in their film debuts, and Fanny MacNamara) challenges social authority embodied in science and patriarchal figures like the misogynist gynecologist.

Simulating the spirit of screwball comedy, *Labyrinth of Passions* is also replete with comic chases—the stepmother pursuing her stepson, the Lacanian psychiatrist in hot sexual pursuit of the woman-hating gynecologist, and, throughout, the persistent gang of Tiranian fundamentalists pursuing Riza to the airport and finally contenting themselves with kidnapping his stepmother.

This disparate blend of international sources—Hollywood comedies, European kitsch love stories, recent world politics transformed into gossip-magazine fare—is all mediated through the notable local mise-en-scène of Madrid during the *movida* period. The credits and opening sequence are set in the Rastro Sunday flea market, in which Riza and Sexilia, still unknown to each other, are prowling the stalls in search of sexual adventure. From an establishing shot that identifies the market area, the camera swiftly cuts to a chain of medium close-ups of crotches and buttocks as the two protagonists vie for the same sexual mates. Thus the Rastro, an emblematic sign of the new Madrid, establishes the urban as the site of the tearing down of scopic and sexual barriers that will eventually lead to important social realignments. Madrid becomes the ubiquitous protagonist of the film, embodying the rejection of figures of patriarchal authority.

This affirmation of Madrid displacing Paris or New York as a cultural model must be read within the logic of the contemporary culture of the decade of Transition. Rejecting the gray city of Francoism and the Europeanism of the cinema of quality, Almodóvar's Madrid introduces us to a street culture that glorifies the youth and drug scene so identified with *La movida*.

The liberated drug and sex culture and the freedom that marks Madrid are embodied in a secondary character played by Almodóvar's real-life performance partner during this period, Fabio de Miguel, a.k.a. Fabio MacNamara or Fanny MacNamara, who appears in the first post-credit sequence reading an article about Patty Diphusa, a famous female impersonator and international porn queen. The article, which we see in close-up, contains a photograph of Patty played by the same Fabio, thus introducing the theme of identity confusion that will be central to the main plot about creative and multiple identities. At the time of the shooting, a *fotonovela* authored by Almodóvar under the nom de plume Patty Diphusa appeared in the Madrid magazine *La Víbora* (1982, nos. 32–33). The tie-in between the character in the film and Almodóvar's literary alter ego further blurred the creative lines between Almodóvar and his filmic world. In the Diphusa writings, the heroine, Patty, a hypersexualized picaresque character, recounts her exploits as an international sex symbol in an episodic structure, revealing herself to be in constant sexual movement.

The equation of the figure of Patty as Almodóvar's alter ego and the link between the film and the broader culture style of *La movida* are made explicit in a later comic scene in which MacNamara poses for images in a *fotonovela* and is directed onscreen by Almodóvar himself. More significant, however, is the figure embodied by MacNamara within the film as a cross-gendered character who reveals the Pygmalian role of Almodóvar as his author. Patty normalizes the blurring of gender and, outside the film, blurs the lines between entertainment and reality. She speaks in the voice of the author just as, in the *fotonovela* shoot scene, MacNamara reveals Almodóvar's authorial manipulation. Ultimately, Patty's importance in relation to *Labyrinth of Passions* lies in the way she embodies a series of themes that will open up Almodóvar's subsequent narrative development. Principal among these are the linkage between the slipperiness of gender identity and the depiction of the post-Franco city as the engine for the emergence of previously marginalized individuals, most notably women and gays.

Migration and Melodrama

What little we see of *La movida madrileña* in Almodóvar's next film, *Entre tinieblas* (Dark Habits; 1983), is the drug culture depicted as background to a narrative that gives more centrality to character development. The film focuses on migration as a pivotal theme and melodrama as the expressive code through which the ideological contradictions of migration are made visible. Almodóvar describes *Dark Habits* as "the film in which for the first time I dared to tell a very sentimental and melodramatic story" (Strauss, *Conversaciones* 42). This and his next film, *¿Qué he hecho yo para merecer esto?* (What Have I Done to Deserve

This?; 1984), offer a culturally specific use of melodrama rooted in the historical experience of Spanish women's survival and self-discovery in the city as they face the crisis of economic and cultural change produced by migration. In the mise-en-scène of these works, the city is the agency through which melodramatic heroines come to embrace Spain's emerging modernity.

Although scholars have extensively treated melodrama in Almodóvar's cinema (see especially excellent discussions by Kinder, *Blood Cinema;* Vernon, "Melodrama against Itself"; and Triana-Toribio, "Almodóvar's Melodramatic *Mise-en-scène*"), the crucial relation of melodrama to the narratives of migration is often ignored. His first two melodramatic heroines, the Mother Superior of *Dark Habits* and Gloria in *What Have I Done to Deserve This?* embody the clash between Spain's traditionalism and cultural modernization. Thomas Elsaesser has generalized the historical rise of melodrama as an expressive mode that corresponded with "periods of intense social and ideological crisis" (45). The tensions of social displacement wrought by decades of steady population shifts from rural and provincial Spain to major urban centers is the symptomatic backstory to the development of these two strongly drawn female protagonists. What we understand retrospectively as Almodóvar's distinctive authorial style is first made legible through the development of melodramatic heroines whose identity has been forged by the crucible of modernity as embodied in the city.

In both films the migration narrative shapes the heroine's psychological crisis. The plot of *Dark Habits* pivots around a congregation of nuns who have come to Madrid from the provincial city of Albacete to save fallen women. The Mother Superior (Julieta Serrano) and her colleagues discover a modern world outside the cloister that redirects each woman's religious zeal to a variety of contemporary obsessions. Narrative conflict is consequently driven by the threat that they will have to close the convent and return to Albacete. In *What Have I Done to Deserve This?* dialogue and action emphasize the problems of social and psychological adjustment to an urban environment for family members who still hold nostalgic views of their rural roots as they struggle to survive in the city.

Marsha Kinder argues that, long before Almodóvar, melodrama served as an organizing principle for a series of ideologically repressive Spanish film scenarios (*Blood* 44–45). She points to Florián Rey's *Aldea maldita* (Damned Village; 1930), the last great silent epic made in Spain, as a paradigmatic expression of the patriarchal melodramatic plot that would reverberate across a body of Spanish films. In Rey's film, economic hard times force the breakup of the family. The immorality of the city further threatens patriarchal authority and is marked as the source of the female's fall into disgrace. A similar and no doubt more familiar version of the migration narrative for Almodóvar is José Antonio Nieves Conde's film *Surcos* (Furrows; 1950), in which the promise of economic improvement for a farm family recently arrived in the city leads to the dissolution of the family. Only when the father reasserts his place and the family returns to the provinces is moral order restored. As Kinder notes in regard to these films, the family becomes the structuring mechanism that organizes all others within Spanish melodramatic discourse.

It is easy to see how Almodóvar could develop his own migration narrative from such a movie tradition. But in his refashioning, far from being the source of destruction of the family, the city is refigured as the place of liberation from the tyrannical sexual and social codes of patriarchy. Madrid, which in his earlier films had been simply the site of a hedonistic liberation, is now the source of the varied emotional rites of passage to modernity for his characters. Discussing the change of tone between these and his two previous films, Almodóvar observes the emotional excess that defines the narratives and the heroines: "'In *Dark Habits* emotions are exposed in a very clear manner. It has a lot of importance in the plot, and the characters are motivated by emotions'" (qtd. in Vidal, *El cine* 67).

While this genealogy of Spanish melodrama and migration situates Almodóvar's films in the historical specificity of Spanish national cinema, he counterbalances the local with reference to American film melodrama as a way to expand his audience and reposition his work in national and transnational contexts. As Kathleen Vernon argues, intertextual citations of American melodrama provide "a vehicle for articulating his distance from the themes and style of a recent Spanish film tradition obsessed with the country's past" ("Melodrama" 59). As he develops a style that opposes Spanish art cinema's predilection for high-culture literary adaptations, even in rural dramas (such as Ricardo Franco's *Pascual Duarte*

[1975], or Mario Camus's *Los santos inocentes* [1983]), he flaunts the popular, low-culture potential of melodrama as a form of address to a broader Spanish audience. He does this through an elaborate chain of intertextual quotes from a variety of well-known Hollywood films.

On a more complex level, the system of Hollywood cinematic citation that begins with American melodrama makes clear what Vernon describes as Almodóvar's "intertextual and international network of references [that serve] to question the role of film itself, not only in reflecting the ideologies and values of the society in which and for which it is created, but also film's complicity in perpetuating those societal structures" ("Melodrama" 60). Vernon points to the subversive use of melodrama to expose the patriarchal structures that have regulated feminine desire. In this regard, melodrama functions not only as a historical index of contemporary culture but also as the model for a style of narration inspired by Hollywood as "the quintessential storyteller" (59).

Dark Habits (1983)

Almodóvar explains the relation between the mise-en-scène of the Madrid convent and his embrace of melodramatic mode of experience: "'For me, *Dark Habits* is completely immersed in the melodramatic genre, with very concrete and clear references to Douglas Sirk, especially in terms of lighting. When I was preparing the film with Ángel Luis Fernández [cinematographer], I gave him cues to light in the Sirk style, but also the chiaroscuros of Zurbarán's paintings. . . . But the melodrama doesn't only come from there. It emerges very directly from the fact that they're talking about love, which has an energy that moves them to do the most extraordinary things, without worrying that at times these may be the most wretched or sublime acts. We're talking about love and passion'" (qtd. in Vidal, *El cine* 73). While some critics read Almodóvar's use of religious iconography as a mere update of Luis Buñuel's anticlericalism, his interest is not in lampooning religious belief but in examining it as an expressive code: "'Religion is the language that human beings have invented for themselves to connect with something superior, and that language contains a series of religious rituals that pass for piety. The paradox of the film is that these women have a religion, but not a religion inspired by God'" (qtd. in Vidal, *El cine* 68–69).

In plotting *Dark Habits*, Almodóvar conceives of his characters and the spaces of their movement as rooted in the "passionate desire [that] lies at the heart of the city" (Triana-Toribio, "Almodóvar's" 182). The storyline initially focuses on Yolanda Bell (Cristina Sánchez Pascual), a heroin-addicted torch singer who goes into hiding when her boyfriend overdoses and dies in her apartment. She is taken in by the Mother Superior of the order of Redentoras Humilladas (Humbled Redeemers), who is one of her most enthusiastic fans. The plot quickly shifts from Yolanda to the Mother Superior, whose melodramatic plight will be an unrequited lesbian desire for Yolanda.

Yolanda's arrival at the convent comes shortly after the Marquesa (Mary Carrillo), the congregation's protectress, has decided to stop supporting the religious order, precipitating certain economic ruin for the congregation. The community of nuns is a motley group of five eccentrics with odd religious names: Sor Rata del Callejón (Sister Alley Rat; Chus Lampreave); Sor Estiércol (Sister Manure; Marisa Paredes); Sor Víbora (Sister Viper; Lina Canelejas); and Sor Perdida (Sister Lost Woman; Carmen Maura). Each of the nuns has a unique obsession: Sor Rata writes bestselling sensationalist sex romances under the name Concha Torres; Sor Víbora, in an amorous relationship with the convent's chaplain (Manuel Zarzo), designs seasonal costume changes for the various religious statues; Sor Perdida cares for the animals in the convent, especially El Niño, a Bengal tiger; Sor Estiércol is in charge of the kitchen and prepares meals that regularly include hard drugs.

The community's economic crisis and the Mother Superior's intensifying passion for Yolanda lead to a narrative climax at the party the nuns have arranged to celebrate the Mother Superior's saint's day. Things do not go well. The Mother General arrives from Albacete and orders the convent shut down. Yolanda goes off with the Marquesa, and in the final scene, the Mother Superior confronts her solitude with a howling shriek as she realizes Yolanda has abandoned her. The film ends with a freeze-frame, shot from outside Yolanda's bedroom, of Sister Manure consoling the Mother Superior, as the voice of Lucho Gatica is heard singing "Encadenados" (Chained).

In Almodóvar's most mature conceptualization of the interrelation of story and characters to date, the interweaving of emotional and social crises predominates. The Marquesa speaks bluntly of the difficult economic times that the country is going through, which will cause her to stop supporting the order and thereby provoke the narrative crisis that shapes the film's plot. Yet that dramatic moment is only an external mark of a more profound drama that has already affected all the members of the religious community. These women have come from Albacete to perform charitable work by providing haven for youthful drug offenders, prostitutes, and murderers. With time, however, it has become apparent that the nuns' "good deeds" are as much a liberation for them from the oppressive, cloistered atmosphere of the provinces as they are a demonstration of Good Samaritanism. In this way, Almodóvar characterizes religious faith as being, at best, a convenient sublimation of individual desire, which in the context of the New Spain has become the catalyst for each woman's self-realization: "More than anything else, this film is about the autonomy of a group of women who confront the established order in a gutsy, natural, and intuitive way. At the point when things around them don't seem to function, they become ferociously independent and take advantage of this situation to realize their inner selves. Just at the point when their purpose for being seems to have disappeared, they claim their maximum autonomy" (Vidal, *El cine* 81–82).

The characterization of the community of nuns seems at first to be an easy parody of one of the pillars of Francoist culture, the ecclesiastic establishment. That impression quickly fades, however, when we see the ways in which the women interact with the world outside the convent. Almodóvar's explanation of that logic clearly alludes to the shifting nature of post-Franco society. Of special note here are two nuns: Sor Rata, who transforms the lives of the convent's fallen women into lurid bestsellers, and Sor Víbora, whose sublimated relation with the chaplain is built around their dressing the various saints. At one point, the chaplain speaks of the film version of *My Fair Lady*, costumed by Cecil Beaton. The popular reworking of the Pygmalion-Galatea myth has an obvious parallel to their desires, as this is, metacinematically, the story of Almodóvar's first creation of psychologically rich New Spanish women whose desires are shaped by the historical changes that have brought them to their current circumstances.

Sor Víbora and Sor Rata's situations reflect the narrative function that guides all of the nuns: they are consumers of the myths of mass-mediated popular culture, and these myths seem to guide their lives and shape their desires. Almodóvar dramatizes this theme here for the first time, and he will continue to develop it over the next decade. As he notes: "There exists a kind of autonomy in the convent, and when the mission of the Humbled Redeemers ceases to function (they have no sinners to redeem), they begin to employ their time in other things. From there we discover their real personality, but they themselves don't realize that reality and, by inertia, they remain in the convent" (Llauradó 11). What they discover is a world of modernity that does not threaten their beliefs but does unsettle social behavior. For the Mother Superior, the confrontation with reality brings an acknowledgment of her lesbian desire, the source of her melodramatic plight.

In this regard, the real achievement of the film is the development of the Mother Superior as a melodramatic heroine within whom religious and melodramatic passions are conflated. We see this clearly in the elaborate depiction of Catholic ritual that marks Yolanda's arrival at the convent. The scene begins as the nuns in the chapel prepare to take communion. The song is a religious chant of devotion to God, the words of which express the slippery distinction between sacred and erotic love that will shortly be enacted. As they sing, the nuns form a line in the aisle and approach the altar and the priest, whose position is the site of the camera. This framing is of strategic importance, for when the rear doors of the chapel fling open, revealing Yolanda standing in the doorway, she appears as if "a divine apparition" (Vidal, *El cine* 75), with the sun's luminous glow surrounding her shadowy presence. The Mother Superior approaches Yolanda, inviting her to participate in the ceremony. As the rear lighting pours into the darkened chapel, it gives Yolanda the appearance of a saintly figure with a halo surrounding her head and body. The voices of the female chorus block out street noises.

This is the first film in which Almodóvar was able to use this kind of tracking shot, and his reaction to it was strong (Strauss, *Conversaciones* 43). Visually, the camera movement, coupled with a growing understanding of the thematic value of mise-en-scène, creates a range of meanings that are largely absent in his previous work. In the reencounter of Yolanda and the Mother Superior, for instance, the blending of the visual and auditory tracks of the convent and the city street suggests a similar interplay between religious fervor that possesses the nuns and the city that magically seems to have delivered Yolanda to the Mother Superior. In this way, the mise-en-scène poses a harmonious interchange between cloistered and urban spaces that situates the melodramatic tale of the Mother Superior's desire for Yolanda within the larger context of Transition culture embodied in the city.

One of the key elements of the scene is the use of music to express emotions that might otherwise be restricted to dialogue. Such emphasis on the expressive range of song is one of the canonical features of cinematic melodrama (Elsaesser 50–51). Though music plays a role in Almodóvar's earlier films, here, for the first time, it is diegetically integrated into the plot as character definition and a form of emotional dialogue. There is a pivotal scene in the convent when the Mother Superior and Yolanda find themselves singing the lyrics of the Lucho Gatica *bolero* "Encadenados" in the Mother Superior's office. The lyrics, understood as a heterosexual lament for the singer's imprisonment in an unrequited love, are thus resemanticized, suggesting, at least for the nun, her unrealizable and prohibited sexual attraction for Yolanda.

Independent of the technical mastery of cinematic narrative practices that *Dark Habits* demonstrates, the real attraction of the film for Almodóvar's fans and critics was the impression it gave of being the continuing work of an agent provocateur. It created a scandal at the Venice Film Festival and was removed from the official competition even as the Italian press praised it. Almodóvar insistently objected to the antireligious readings of *Dark Habits*. "I wasn't trying to tear down the religious establishment, which, by the way, I despise. That was not my intention. Absolutely to the contrary, the film follows, at least my idea was to follow closely, in an objective fashion, everything that Christian teaching advocates, the message of Christ when he came to earth, if it is that he came" (Alabadejo 67). The anti-Catholic reading of *Dark Habits* was perhaps an effort by film critics and audiences outside of Spain to understand Almodóvar's film in the context of Buñuel, the most famous Spanish anti-Catholic filmmaker. His protests notwithstanding, the film launched Almodóvar's international career, with Venice critics and the Italian press characterizing him as a figure who debunks one of the essential emblems of traditional Spain, the church.

Retrospectively, commentators have viewed the treatment of Catholic ritual and iconography in this and later Almodóvar films as part of an aesthetic of kitsch (Yarza 50–52). In describing the film's equation of religious ritual with kitsch, Almodóvar observes: "The kitsch aesthetic appears in all of my films, and it's inseparable from religious practice. . . . I used religion to speak of typically human feelings. What interests me, what fascinates me, what moves me in religious practice is its capacity to create a community among people. . . . I transform religious language into profoundly human and amorous language. For me, the most interesting aspect of religion is its theatricality" (Strauss, *Conversaciones* 45).

Ultimately, the value of *Dark Habits* is less the matter of kitsch and camp than the forging of Almodóvar's first powerful melodramatic heroine. In the film's final scene, the transformation of emotion into melodramatic theatricality becomes a profound starting point for a series of heroines who transcend the topical and geographical limits within which Almodóvar's cinema had operated up to this point.

Dark Habits became a modest commercial success in Spain, and Almodóvar began to achieve notoriety as a "bad-boy" director, appearing to expand the range of his treatment of taboo subjects. This is, in a sense, the moment at which the director began in earnest his transformation into an international celebrity filmmaker, approaching the status of auteur. On the basis of the national and international success of the film, Almodóvar started appearing on Spanish television and was able to receive partial financial backing for his next project, which was to be produced by Tesauro Films.

What Have I Done to Deserve This? (1984)

There is a scene about midway through *What Have I Done to Deserve This?* in which Toni, the older son of the film's much-put upon heroine, Gloria (Carmen Maura), goes with his grandmother to see Elia Kazan's 1960 psycho-melodrama *Splendor in the Grass*. In the scene depicted, the first of numerous interpolated films-within-films for Almodóvar, Warren Beatty tells his oil-baron father that he would rather work on a farm than go to college. Speaking of a similar film-within-the-film scene in his next work, *Matador* (1986), Almodóvar says that when the protagonists of that film go to the movies to see King Vidor's *Duel in the Sun*, "[T]hey look at the screen and they see their future. . . . When you go to the cinema, the cinema reflects not your life but your end"

(Kinder, "Pleasure" 41). On a broader, self-referential level, the film-within-the-film device suggests the power of the cinematic medium to awaken individual and collective desires.

The interpolated movie scene in *What Have I Done to Deserve This?* prepares the audience for the denouement, in which Toni and his grandmother return to their native village. More importantly, it works with an array of other cinematic quotes to form a mode of address to the film's audience. Taken collectively as a single discursive strategy, these intertextual citations constitute Almodóvar's most radical reformulation to date of the storytelling process in his films. They are used to refine and resemanticize the concepts of migration and melodrama that he began to explore in *Dark Habits*. This is a "purposeful eclecticism" in cinematic citation (Vernon, "Melodrama" 59) that reveals its own narrative and thematic coherence as a way to mirror what Peter W. Evans calls "the underlying principle of cultural heterogeneity" at work in Spain in the 1980s ("Amodóvar's" 326). The filmic citations from Spanish and Hollywood movies that punctuate the narrative are all rooted in one of two axes of cultural meaning: migration or melodrama. Melodrama holds a special privilege as a structuring discourse, a form of address to the film's multiple audiences.

These self-references reposition the all-too-familiar story of emotional and social dislocation in the city, one of the primary social narratives of modern Spain, within a larger geocultural context. As Kinder persuasively demonstrates, opposition filmmakers of the 1950s, such as Bardem and Berlanga, often combined opposing filmic styles, specifically Hollywood melodrama and Italian neorealism, as a dialectical counterpoint, with the aim of distinguishing their work from the discourse of official cultural representation (*Blood* 36–37). In his specific choices of textual quotes in *What Have I Done to Deserve This?* Almodóvar acknowledges the heterogeneity of contemporary Spanish culture through the mixing of Spanish and Hollywood movie references. Even more importantly, as Núria Triana-Toribio argues, he uses the melodramatic mise-en-scène as a visual-aural narrational apparatus through which to tell his story: "Thus the function of the mise-en-scène and the music is crucial as it allows economy of narration and aids in the development of a steady succession of narrative elements that advance the action . . . we should look at objects, clothes, make-up, and song as if they were them-

Almodóvar directing Francisca Caballero
(his mother) and Chus Lampreave in a scene
from *What Have I Done to Deserve This?*
Courtesy of the Filmoteca Española.

selves narrators, albeit ambiguous ones" ("Almodóvar's" 179–80). In this
regard, the film marks a crucial advance in Almodóvar's understanding
of the material practices of cinema that enables him to further develop
a coherent cultural narrative.

The story is set in the specific urban space of Madrid's Barrio de
la Concepción, a working-class district of monstrous high-rise slums
constructed as part of Franco's housing plan of the 1960s in belated
response to decades of continuous rural migrations to Spain's major
cities. For Spanish audiences, this mise-en-scène mirrors the migration
narrative that is a constant refrain from various characters, but most
particularly the grandmother (Chus Lampreave). Although the plot is
devilishly complex, its underlying logic clearly parallels that of Nieves
Conde's *Surcos,* a film Almodóvar acknowledges as one of the cinematic
inspirations for *What Have I Done?* In this intricately braided narrative, Gloria, the downtrodden housewife, struggles to make ends meet
by working outside the home as a cleaning woman. Gloria lives in a

cluttered little apartment with her brutish husband, Antonio (Ángel de Andrés-Lopez), her two sons, Toni and Miguel, and Antonio's mother, who hates the cold city and pines to return to her native village. Years earlier, Antonio had been a guest worker in Germany, but he is now reduced to driving a cab.

The family's fragile economic status has had an obvious impact on their two sons. Toni is a drug pusher, and his younger brother Miguel sleeps with his friend's father. To survive in this anguished situation, Gloria pops tranquilizers and sniffs cleaning fluids. She manages to get money for a curling iron by allowing Miguel to be "adopted" by the boy's pedophile dentist. Jealousy emerges as a mere detail in Gloria's unhappy marriage when Lucas (Gonzalo Suárez), a writer, involves Antonio in a get-rich-quick scheme to bring Ingrid Müller (Katia Loritz), Antonio's old German flame and purported lover to Adolph Hitler, to Madrid to forge a volume of Hitler's love letters. In the midst of a domestic argument, Gloria hits Antonio on the head with a ham bone and kills him. In the aftermath of Antonio's death, Gloria finds herself in near total solitude. After her mother-in-law returns to the country with Toni, she even contemplates suicide, but, just in the nick of time, Miguel returns to the house to take charge.

Various details of this plot reinforce the motif of movement and the backstories of migration. The apartment block where Gloria lives is situated on the edge of the monster expressway, the M-30, continually underscoring images of movement. Details of Antonio's migratory biography are gradually revealed through dialogue: his experience as a guest worker in Germany in the "Happy Sixties," his return to his village, and the subsequent move with his family to the tiny flat in Madrid. His mother's longing to return to the *pueblo* is finally achieved after Antonio's death. The grandmother's frequent encounters with a neighbor from the village (Francisca Caballero, Almodóvar's mother) further reinforce the connection between migration and exilic nostalgia. Among the other comings and goings in the plot, Cristal (Verónica Forqué), the prostitute next door, dreams of going to Las Vegas to be a star. Paul Julian Smith speaks of another neighbor, Juani (Kiti Manver), whose Jaén accent "constantly reaffirm[s] the presence of the country in the city (*Desire* 57). This is all part of a process of historical nostalgia, a gesture never so overtly posed in his prior films. There is, for instance, Antonio's mother's collecting of tree branches that remind her of her village and even her musical nostalgia, as she pines upon hearing Miguel de Molina's voice entoning "La Bien Pagá" (The Well-Paid Woman): "How beautiful the songs were back in my day!" This nostalgia deepens the presumed pastiche of Almodóvar's style, as it is now grounded in the ambivalence of a Spanish urban space still in the throes of modernization.

As in Néstor García Canclini's notion of "hybrid cultures," characters are continually entering and leaving modernity, returning to the *pueblo* to retrieve nostalgic mementos (332–33). Nostalgia linked to migration is a motif more broadly generalized in Spanish literature of the early twentieth century, as Noël Valis remind us: "[It] issues out of the geographic sense of place and only later becomes interiorized as the place within the individual psyche" (207).

This temporal ambivalence is apparent in Almodóvar's masterful construction of the Dantesque urban mise-en-scène of the Barrio de la Concepción, which commentators have seen as a clear link with Italian neorealism as well as analogous to the urban spaces in Spanish neorealist films. Almodóvar describes it, however, as akin to the cityscape of Ridley Scott's futuristic *Blade Runner* (D'Lugo 133). Retrospectively, he acknowledges another spiritual link to a countercultural Spanish cinematic tradition, the bittersweet offshoot of Italian neorealism known as Spanish "black comedies" of the late 1950s and early 1960s. Films like Marco Ferreri's *El cochecito* (The Little Car; 1960) and Berlanga's *Plácido* (1961) and *El verdugo* (The Executioner; 1962), as well as Fernando Fernán Gómez's *El extraño viaje* (The Strange Journey; 1963), were later acknowledged by Almodóvar as essential precursors to his films (Strauss, *Conversaciones* 55). These black comedies came out of a specific historical context in which, after decades of economic privation, Spaniards were beginning to experience the first taste of consumerist culture that had been the promise of Franco's economic policies. In the late 1950s and early 1960s the government began to respond to the housing crisis with apartment blocks such as those seen in the film. *What Have I Done to Deserve This?* picks up on that critique of consumerist culture with a biting sense of humor, as when Gloria effectively trades her son Miguel for a curling iron, or when Antonio is recruited to counterfeit Hitler's love letters.

Such social history notwithstanding, the centerpiece of the film is the melodramatic character of Gloria. She assumes narrative centrality from the beginning, suggesting a firmer initial conception than *Dark Habits*, in which the Mother Superior only gradually emerges from a chorus of colorful characters. Carmen Maura was not Almodóvar's first choice for the role; he had originally hoped to have Esperanza Roy play Gloria. When she was unavailable, he was reluctant to call on Maura, since in her earlier work with him (*Pepi, Luci, Bom* and *Dark Habits*), there had been little indication of the powerful dramatic depth she would bring to the role.

Maura and Almodóvar both claim that Gloria was not supposed to be a "funny" character. As Maura notes, this is the first Almodóvar film in which she doesn't appear to have any comic lines (Vidal, *El cine* 127). The humor is built upon a distanced tragicomic quality in her indomitable spirit that reveals vulnerability as well as strength. The first post-credit narrative sequence parodies the famous image from Hitchcock's *Psycho*. During a casual sexual encounter with a policeman (Luis Hostelot) in the showers at a Kendo parlor, Gloria is viewed in a high-angle shot from the point of view of the shower nozzle, frantically struggling against the inevitability of sexual frustration as the officer loses his erection. Remaining behind as the male clients file out, Gloria picks up one of the Kendo lances and lunges forward with a grunt in imitation of what she has witnessed. It is a sound and gesture that acknowledges her frustration but, even more significantly, asserts its own phallic force. Sexual frustration is later generalized in her obligatory lovemaking with Antonio and in a vignette when Cristal asks her to please a customer by serving as a voyeur audience when Cristal makes love with him. All three scenes point to the impotence of patriarchal figures: the police, the husband, and the male consumer of sex. In the voyeuristic scene with Cristal, Gloria's deadpan expression in the face of the male's vain illusion of power underscores her comic detachment from the world around her.

Similarly, during Antonio's selfish lovemaking with Gloria, her expression remains indifferent to her husband's version of sexual pleasure. The offscreen music is "La bien pagá," the 1940s song whose lyrics pose a bitter and ironic commentary on Gloria's predicament. Equally ironic is the onscreen image of Almodóvar himself dressed in a red hussar's uniform lip-synching the words to his nightclub partner, Fanny Mac-

Namara, dressed as Scarlett O'Hara. This is a camp moment, but one that reinforces the multiple scenarios of coupling and of the status of women, conspicuously those of wife and prostitute. If Gloria is to be paired with Scarlett O'Hara, it will be through the insistence on her indomitable spirit. Yet the ironic cross-dressing of MacNamara suggests that Gloria's survival will require a regendering of her femininity if she is to succeed. Through her evolving dramatic range, first in the role of Gloria and later as Tina in *Law of Desire* and Pepa in *Women on the Verge of a Nervous Breakdown*, Maura underscores the notion that gender is not a simple biological polarity. As David Leavitt remarks, "Being a woman in Almodóvar's movies is more a state of mind than a state of chromosomes" (40).

Here, as at other moments in the film, Almodóvar mobilizes melodramatic strategies to narrate the heroine's plight. Maria LaPlace has argued that one staple of Hollywood's women's melodrama is fetishized commodity consumption (139). Gloria finds herself at the center of the consumerist nightmare that gradually comes into focus as one of the driving forces of the film's melodramatic plot. As Vernon notes, Almodóvar places Gloria in a "conventional kitchen setting, the camera portrays the protagonist in a series of reverse-angle shots, a classical editing figure. . . . The camera is positioned to show the appliances, in effect, looking back at her. . . . TV commercials for clothes washers and fried chicken recipes long ago appropriated this particular editing figure" ("Melodrama" 66). Similarly, when she first views the curling iron for which she will trade her son Miguel, the camera tracks her movement on the street in an intricate panning that suggests that the objects in store windows are looking back at her. The subject object conflation does much to underscore the degraded position that Gloria occupies in the consumerist illusion of a Spanish working class for whom the dream of cultural modernization in post-Franco Spain is at best a moot topic and at worst a mean trick.

The parodies of the melodramatic heroine as consumer identify Gloria as a Spanish clone of the consumerist works evoked from the various Hollywood melodrama citations. These are juxtaposed against a series of Spanish cinematic intertexts that similarly repositions Gloria's story within the history of Spanish films that challenged the Francoist image of traditional culture. These include the cameo appearance of two art-film directors of the period, Gonzalo Suárez and Jaime Chávarri. Suárez plays Lucas, the would-be porn novelist, and Chávarri appears in the outrageous role of one of Cristal's customers, an exhibitionist who requires an audience for his striptease and his lovemaking. In addition, Almodóvar features two actors identified with the social realist cinema of the 1960s and 1970s: Amparo Soler Leal, as Lucas's alcoholic wife Patricia (Triana-Toribio, "¿Qué he hecho?" 229); and Emilio Gutiérrez Caba, one of the faces of the "New Spanish Cinema" of the 1960s (see Saura's *La caza,* 1965; and Patino's *Nueve cartas a Berta,* 1965), who plays Lucas's bother. As Núria Triana-Toribio points out, these narrowly defined cinematic self-references produce a historical discourse to trigger in viewers' minds the nostalgia of a cinematic tradition that was critical of Spanish culture and social circumstances.

What Have I Done to Deserve This? boasted Almodóvar's largest budget to date, seventy million pesetas, still modest according to the patterns of the industry of the time. The film received mixed reviews among Spanish critics, many of whom echoed their earlier complaints about the director's lack of skills in the basics of writing and directing (Edwards 42). As a telling sign of things to come, however, while the government's Ministry of Culture was lauding Mario Camus's adaptation of Miguel Delibes's novel *Los santos inocentes* (Holy Innocents), which won important acting awards at Cannes in 1983, *What Have I Done?* was being shown to appreciative audiences as part of the New York Museum of Modern Art's "New Directors Series." The film received notable praise from Pauline Kael in the *New Yorker,* who commented on its offbeat humor. *What Have I Done?* became Almodóvar's first solid international hit. Distributed in Italy, it was invited to the 1985 Montreal Film Festival, and its U.S. release occasioned flattering reviews from the *New York Times* and *Village Voice.*

Such a positive critical reaction from American film circles served as an obvious form of authentication for Almodóvar that was all but lacking for him in Spain. Over the next three years, as his films came to embrace a more pronounced personal authorial style, they would also move toward a model that would be more easily marketable within U.S. distribution circuits and closer to what would appear to many critics as a Hollywood style of film.

Thrillers

Almodóvar's fifth feature-length film, *Matador* (1986), was coproduced under the auspices of Andrés Vicente Gómez's Iberoamericana Films and RTVE, Spanish State Television. Taking advantage of special subsidies from the Ministry of Culture's Miró law (named for the director of the socialist government's Film Office who spearheaded the policy of energetic government film subventions), the production received a subvention against future box-office receipts. Gómez was able to provide Almodóvar with his largest budget to date (some 120 million pesetas, of which over half was provided by the government subsidy), which led to a more technically polished "look" than any of his earlier films. In exchange for such support, however, Almodóvar would have to adapt to the Gómez production model, which would definitively alter his cinematic style and send him in a creative direction only hinted at in his earlier work.

During the 1980s, Gómez was a trailblazer within Spanish production circles for his belief in the potential exportability of Spanish quality cinema (Gómez 70). He followed strategies introduced by Elías Querejeta, who internationalized Spanish auteur cinema in the 1960s and 1970s with films by Carlos Saura and Víctor Erice through a series of government subsidies and clever marketing abroad. Gómez cultivated promising directors whose work he considered exportable. Some, like Saura, were already well-established filmmakers with international reputations. Others, like Fernando Trueba, José Juan Bigas Luna, and Pedro Almodóvar, had gained national attention and appeared ripe for Gómez's type of exploitation. Gómez brokered three such projects in 1985: Trueba's *El año de las luces* (The Year of Lights); Bigas Luna's *Lola;* and Almodóvar's project, tentatively titled *Lo inevitable* (The Inevitable), which, at Gómez's suggestion, was retitled *Matador.*

In many ways the pairing of Almodóvar with Gómez's operation was ideal, since Gómez was interested in films that revised and updated traditional Spanish cultural icons with an eye to marketing these films internationally. For his part, Almodóvar had been steadily moving toward a strong self-conscious rewriting of the marks of Spanish cultural identity, particularly as they related to themes of traditional patriarchal culture and comic treatments of previously taboo sex themes. With *Matador*, this tendency intensified and was aligned more conspicuously with Hollywood genre films, especially melodrama and the thriller. The Gómez patronage effectively reframed the local filmmaker as a transnational auteur through the refiguring of Spanish culture itself. Further, it gave Almodóvar a decisive lesson in the international promotion of his films, planting the seeds for the subsequent founding of his own production company, El Deseo S.A. The collaboration with Gómez, however, eventually proved unworkable. Almodóvar wanted a producer who would give him his undivided attention during production; Gómez liked coordinating two or even three projects simultaneously. Thus, the two men agreed to sever their contractual arrangements after *Matador* (Gómez 53).

Consistent with the lessons learned from Gómez, *Matador* and the subsequent *La ley del deseo* (Law of Desire) depicted a Madrid that was visually striking and modern, a far cry from the drab though raucous city of Almodóvar's earlier films. To some degree, the change might also reflect his first collaboration with another scriptwriter. Up to this point, he had been the sole author of his scripts. For *Matador*, however, he worked with Jesús Ferrero, principally on dialogue for a number of scenes: "Jesús Ferrero helped me find the words to transform this Latin drama into something more Japanese or more universal" (Vidal, *El cine* 159). Strikingly, one of the essential "concepts" of the film was to take icons and emblems of Spanish culture, such as bullfighting and religion, which were part of the folkloric repertory Almodóvar had been developing, and match them with more universally accessible features.

Matador is the first Almodóvar film in which male characters assume a central role in the action, thus serving as a precursor to a series of other male-centered narratives beginning more than a decade later with *Live Flesh* (1997), *Talk to Her* (2002), and *Bad Education* (2004). Though the film was produced before *Law of Desire*, *Matador* was actually scripted after it. Both films share a common narrative-visual dynamic related to sexualized cultural identities. Each also features a self-referential treatment of film genres, especially the Hollywood noir thriller that introduces a world in which gender is interrogated and shifting definitions of sexual identity contest traditional Spanish notions of heterosexual society.

Of the origins of *Matador,* Almodóvar says: "What I wanted to do was to talk about death and its relation to sexuality, and I needed a profession that would be physically related to death, and, rather than a doctor or an anesthetist, which are not really involved with sexuality, I chose a *torero,* who does play with death sensuously and is more active" (Alabadejo 80). Sex and the eroticization of public spaces in the film diminish the particularities of bullfighting in much the same way that, fifteen years later, when Almodóvar returned to this same cluster of themes in *Talk to Her,* a similar breaking down of gender borders will occur in a story that again poses a love theme that defies social conventions and morality.

The storytelling mechanism of *Matador* is streamlined in ways that break with Almodóvar's earlier choral films. Secondary plots and characters are reduced, and there is a more conventional sense of Hollywood-style narrative unity. Diego Montes (Nacho Martínez), a bullfighter who has prematurely retired after being gored in the ring, now runs a school for aspiring *toreros.* Unable to give up the thrill of killing, he has shifted his attention from bulls to young women, whom he murders at the moment of sexual climax. One of his pupils, Ángel (Antonio Banderas), suffers from vertigo and is tormented by his widowed mother (Julieta Serrano) and her obsessive Opus Dei conservative Catholicism. Ángel's neighbor is Eva Soler (Eva Cobo), a fashion model and Diego's girlfriend. To prove to Diego that he is not gay, Ángel attempts to rape Eva, but he fails miserably. He now wants to confess his crime, not to a priest, but to the local police.

In the process of his confession to Inspector Del Valle (Eusebio Poncela), Ángel also claims responsibility for a chain of serial murders. María Cardenal (Assumpta Serna), Ángel's court-appointed attorney, shares with him a common interest in Diego. She is, in fact, the perpetrator of two of the murders being investigated by the police. Seducing her victims in the style of a bullfighter, she gores them in the neck with a long hairpin at the moment of sexual climax. Defending Ángel, she hopes, will bring her closer to Diego. For his part, the bullfighter is intrigued by María and pursues her to a movie theater where they finally meet face to face.

Their fatal attraction is interrupted by Del Valle who, continuing his investigation of the serial murders, becomes interested in Diego's school, since two of the victims were students there. The inspector is certain that Diego is the killer. María learns of this and is further enticed by the image of Diego as her soulmate. Dreaming of the prospect of making love with and then killing him, she invites him to her cottage, decorated as a shrine not only to bullfighting but more specifically to Diego. The two realize that they are destined for each other.

In the meantime, Ángel is being treated by a psychiatrist, Julia (Carmen Maura), who discovers that her patient is subject to trances in which he can see killings being committed elsewhere in the city. This explains his identification with the murders he claims to have committed. Aided by Ángel's powers of foresight, Inspector Del Valle tracks Diego to María's cottage, only to arrive just as they reach simultaneous orgasm and kill each other at the exact moment of a solar eclipse.

As critics have often noted when dealing with the representation of bullfighting in post-Franco cinema, the *corrida* embodies "cultural, economic, religious, and psychosexual fetishism" (Lev 73). Like the fashion show in which Eva appears, the New Spain, by contrast, represents a sexually liberating albeit violent rejection of that past. Although characters never directly refer to the previous regime, in all their actions, dress, talk, and interactions with one another, they are understood as standing in opposition to the Old Spain of Francoism. Peter W. Evans argues that "*Matador,* like all Almodóvar's films, is double-focused: while it looks backwards for historical and ideological rationales of its sexual and political traumas, it looks forward . . . to a society unafraid to speak the names of its multifarious desires" ("Almodóvar's" 330). Much of the film's forward-looking strategy lies in its embrace of international cultural details embodied in the characters' dress and the development of urban space as a cosmopolitan mise-en-scène.

As a backdrop to this new national narrative, the film refigures Madrid as a site of chic contemporary fashion. In a cameo appearance as the fashion designer Francisco Montesinos, Almodóvar explains to a reporter that his fashion show is entitled "Spain Divided," a reference to the ways in which twentieth-century Spanish writers and thinkers have described the tension between traditional values and the struggle for cultural and political modernization. He mockingly characterizes the two Spains as "either envious or intolerant," suggesting that somber and introspective visions of Spain have given way to a more lighthearted and colorful self-image.

The notion of the New Spain as a fashion show underscores not only the secular rituals that have defined Spain and Spanishness as the registers through which Spaniards perform their new identities for the outside world but also the way they have come to see themselves. The spectacle of Spain as an enticing, quasi-exotic, but also chic performance for the cosmopolitan international audience is the engine that self-consciously moves the plot.

Interestingly, the *corrida de toros* is never in itself a sufficient narrative focus. Almodóvar needs to refigure this hoariest of traditional symbols of Spain to represent a ritual of aggressive sexuality far more intense and explicit than any of the latent sexual meanings to which commentators often refer. From the opening credit sequence, the *corrida* is characterized as a heterosexual ritual and a metaphor of the dispersive eroticism that lies beyond the bullring in the public spaces of everyday life. The credits begin with Diego masturbating as he views video images of women's bodies being horribly mutilated. Almodóvar explains the economy of expression of the scene: "With that image I explain that this man gets excited with the image of women dying violently and that he is all alone. He doesn't share his pleasure with anyone" (Vidal, *El cine* 167). The scene ends with a cut to Diego's tauromachy class in which he gives lessons on the "art of killing," the final "moment of truth." Though beginning in his school, the image quickly shifts to María's seduction, copulation with, and murder of a stranger she has picked up on a public square, accompanied by Diego's voiceover commentary on the matador's art. In this way, the film's narrative axis—the pairing of María and Diego in a bond of sexualized death—is succinctly established.

By bringing the spectator into the erotic spectacle, Almodóvar engages his audience in the same kind of erotic visual pleasures that the two protagonists have enjoyed. It may dawn on us only retrospectively that Ángel's "trances," in which he has witnessed and believes he has participated in Diego's and María's murderous seductions, are merely the vicarious guilty pleasures of a sexually repressed young man. Like the androgynous image of the traditional matador that Almodóvar exploits, Ángel's pleasure is suggestively androgynous as well. When he makes his confessions of murder to Inspector Del Valle, he variously describes these bloody seductions from either María's or Diego's point of view, thus suggesting an ambiguous sexual orientation. Like Diego and Del

Valle, we are never sure whether Ángel is discovering his homosexual desire or merely acting out a polymorphous sexuality. This condition is echoed in a line earlier in the film when Diego follows María into the movie-theater bathroom. She confronts him by asking why he is following her. He responds, "This is the men's room," to which she immediately retorts: "Don't trust appearances." In this environment, Ángel's sexual ambivalence seems a metaphor for Spanish culture torn between tradition and modernity.

Of that gender ambiguity, Almodóvar notes: "'María Cardenal and Diego Montes comprise a grand *corrida* in which their roles are interchangeable according to the moment. There are moments when she is the bullfighter and vice versa, as in life there are times when one has masculine or feminine comportment, depending on the situation, although the essence of every individual is clear. Assumpta [María] is almost always the one who takes the initiative in the crimes'" (qtd. in Vidal, *El cine* 166).

The international refiguration of Spanish culture is nonetheless situated in a visual and narrative tension, with the melodrama of the traditional Spanish family in crisis and what Evans calls "the obligatory counter-family (e.g. the school of tauromachy here, but also, for instance, the *movida* world of *Pepi* and *Laberinto de pasiones,* or the gay/transsexual family of *La ley del deseo*)" ("Almodóvar's" 326). One of the film's pivotal expressions of the tension between tradition and modernity is the pairing of Ángel and Eva and their two mothers, who embody the mentality of the old and new order, respectively. Julieta Serrano, who plays Ángel's mother, Berta, is the comic embodiment of ultraconservative Opus Dei Catholicism, a narrative twist that will shape the notion of guilt, which Almodóvar calls the other major theme of *Matador.* Berta spies on her son, even when he is in the bathroom; she berates him at every opportunity, twisting his words into a tirade against her deceased husband and the depravity of post-Franco Spanish morality.

By contrast, Eva's mother, Pilar, is played by Chus Lampreave, who had previously been the conservative mother-in-law to Gloria in *What Have I Done to Deserve This?* She is now ironically cast as the embodiment of the liberal and supportive maternal spirit that Almodóvar identifies with Spain's "alternative non-conformist traditions" (Evans, "Almodóvar's" 328). An elegantly dressed woman, she spouts salty retorts to police detectives, her daughter, and even to Ángel, whom she chides for attempting to rape her daughter. In a telling gesture that underscores the refiguring of the Old Spain into a modern and stylish culture, Pilar leaves her daughter's preparation for the fashion show ostensibly to take her seat in the audience. Instead, she walks onto the stage and catwalk, moving and pausing as though she were a model in the show. Tracing what has become, by this point, the cult status of Lampreave in Almodóvar's films, one may begin to appreciate how, in microcosm, she comes to embody the miraculous transformation of certain positive values of the old order, as in *What Have I Done?* into a new maternalism and a new cosmopolitan identity.

Pilar and Berta are thus set up as symbolic rivals in the plot, crystallizing the film's thematic opposition: The project of contemporizing Spain is posed as a series of images and icons and a way of being in the film that rejects the Francoist past and seeks to rewrite its underlying social and personal values. We note this in the insistence on costume and color in the mise-en-scène, as it suggests the openness and beauty of the city (especially shots of the elegant areas near the Plaza de Oriente) and its inhabitants that are in radical contrast to the image of Madrid and *madrileños* depicted in *What Have I Done?* (Vidal, *El cine* 168; García de León and Maldonado 133).

Evans notes that, while playing up some other modes of Hollywood genres, especially film noir, "*Matador* re-creates the classic Hollywood melodrama's formulae both in its dependence on traditional family narratives and in the resonant hyperboles of its baroque form" ("Almodóvar's" 328). In *Matador*, the family melodrama is lodged in the male rather than the female victim, as embodied in the Antonio Banderas character, Ángel. In Banderas's first prominent film appearance, his character comes to embody the negative power of repressive Spanish Catholic education (Alabadejo 80). Guilt and humiliation for sins real and imagined has been so drummed into Ángel by his tyrannical mother that, in a comic twist, he confesses to all the murders actually committed by María and Diego. Almodóvar reveals that his character was inspired by the guilt-ridden characters of Hitchcock films and Patricia Highsmith novels (Vidal, *El cine* 175). Although his presence guides the murder mystery, Ángel is less the focus of action than a conduit to frame the figure of the monstrous mother, whose religious fanaticism has scarred her son.

This cluster of themes of religious fanaticism and the castrating Spanish mother serves as a historical background to the dynamic representation of Spanish modernization that the film expounds in the quirky pairing of Diego, María, and Eva. In the overt and subtle cinematic quotes from Hollywood genre films, as embedded in the self-referential cinematic characterizations of his protagonists, Almodóvar does not seek to create a Spanish imposter version of genre films in *Matador* but, as in *What Have I Done to Deserve This?* to interrogate forms of social identity that have been circulated through dominant media representations.

The production qualities, soundtrack, costume, and image all contribute to the first conscious effort to market an Almodóvar film internationally. Paul Julian Smith notes that at various points in the film Almodóvar exploits the tension between the "idealistic shibboleth of the 'Iberian character' and the sterile impersonality of joyless internationalism" (Smith, *Desire* 76). Spanishness is seen as a performance within which identity is highly changeable, as in a fashion show. In the final scene, Smith notes a kind of "historical fetish," which, like sexual fetish, serves "to protect the subject from the wounds of history" by emphasizing the cinematic mise-en-scène (76).

Ironically, with all of its self-conscious treatment of Spanish traditional icons as they are reread in modernity, *Matador* was not initially appealing to distributors outside of Spain, failing to even match the receipts of *What Have I Done to Deserve This?* in its domestic run, although it did reasonably well (112 million pesetas). Not until the powerful crossover effect of *Law of Desire* did *Matador* get major distribution elsewhere. The success of *Law of Desire* generated interest in Antonio Banderas, who is only a supporting actor in *Matador*. In both films he is cast as a violence-prone repressed homosexual, but this did not seem to hurt his international appeal.

Law of Desire (1987)

Law of Desire is the first film to be produced by Almodóvar's own company, formed in collaboration with his brother Agustín, which afforded him a new degree of creative control. Other Spanish filmmakers had gone this same route, most notably Fernando Colomo, José Luis Borau, Fernando Trueba, and Imanol Uribe. Almodóvar's notable distribution success may be attributed to the collaboration with Agustín, whose business acumen was balanced with a sensitivity to his brother's artistic needs and a keen sense of the markets to which El Deseo's films could be directed. The recent experience of working with Andrés Vicente Gómez on *Matador,* which Agustín noted had been "sold" before the film was even released (Vidal, *El cine* 246), suggested a model for the financing and distribution of their films that was sorely needed as Pedro's career evolved: "With my first five films I had the impression of having had five children with five different fathers and of always fighting with each one of them, since my films belonged to them, from a financial point of view, but also on an artistic level, that is, on the level of a conception" (Strauss, *Conversaciones* 64).

Though written before *Matador,* *Law of Desire* was produced after its international release. By an ironic turn of events, however, the international distribution of *Law of Desire* as a gay film preceded the U.S. premiere of *Matador,* leading Pauline Kael to remark as she reviewed *Matador* and *High Heels* in the *New Yorker* that Almodóvar's movies were opening in reverse order (466). This point gives credence to the argument that Almodóvar's international status was first secured through the promotion of his films as gay cinema (Mandrell 42). One essential feature of the Gómez collaboration was the realization that a film could be tailored to join multiple audiences. In the creative development of *Law of Desire,* Almodóvar begins to shape an international formula.

The dominant international images of Spain's cinema during the mid-1980s were emblemized by the films of Carlos Saura, most conspicuously in the recent international success of *Carmen.* Saura and his film constituted traditional cultural capital for the promotion of Spanish cinema abroad: an established and much-honored auteur and subject matter that reflected a privileged national cultural patrimony. As Núria Triana-Toribio reminds us, the Miró law was intended to promote the international distribution of Spanish films, but its authors were especially opposed to comedies and melodramas as inappropriate cinematic vehicles through which to export Spanish culture (*Spanish* 138). After the international success of *What Have I Done to Deserve This?* Almodóvar's films were seen to be potentially fundable as exportable national cinema. Though Gómez had easily gotten a subvention for the production of *Matador,* the first attempts to get financial support for *Law of Desire* from the Ministry of Culture had been unsuccessful. It was only through the intervention of subsecretary Fernando Méndez-Leite that the subsidy was arranged (Vidal, *El cine* 245). The hundred-million-peseta budget made it a more modest production than *Matador.* Thirty-eight million pesetas were provided by an advance subsidy from the Ministry of Culture, and another twenty million from the Ministry of Industry (Boquerini 88).

Law of Desire would be the first film to challenge the government's conception of exportable, transnational Spanish cinema. In an influential interview in *Film Quarterly* in the fall of 1987, Marsha Kinder asked Almodóvar if he could explain the international appeal of his films, especially *Law of Desire,* which had recently been a resounding critical success in Europe and the United States. He responded: "I think my films are very contemporary. They represent more than others, I suppose, the New Spain, this kind of new mentality that appears after Franco dies, especially after 1977 till now" ("Pleasure" 36).

Among its many distinctions, *Law of Desire* is also the first Almodóvar film in which movies and cinematic self-reference are central to the plot. While a metacinematic thread clearly runs through the early films—including Pepi's brief interest in videotaping the biographies of Luci and Bom, the staging of the filmmaking process in the initial shot of the precredits of *What Have I Done to Deserve This?* and in Diego and María's viewing of their destiny in King Vidor's *Duel in the Sun.* In *Law of Desire,* however, cinema becomes an integral part of the plot.

Although some commentators have attempted to read Almodóvar's autobiography into the film, the more significant aspect of the cinematic self-reference lies in the way the film links cinematic creation to the questions of identity construction. Pablo Quintero (Eusebio Poncela), a gay filmmaker, has adapted the life of his transsexual sister, Tina (Carmen Maura), into a film script. Pablo has altered the name of the heroine to Laura P., a name that will circulate within the complex narrative that unravels around the two siblings. Pablo has asked his lover, Juan (Miguel Molina), who is working in a bar in Cádiz for the summer, to mail him a letter that Pablo has composed as an example of the kind of love letter he wants to receive. This letter introduces the motif of recycled identities. Juan mails the letter, which is read by Antonio (Antonio Banderas), a repressed youth who has been stalking Pablo and who, in turn, is seduced by Pablo. While rummaging through Pablo's papers, Antonio comes across the script of Laura P.'s biography. He later asks Pablo to write him a love letter, but to sign it Laura P. because of his suspicious mother.

Antonio quickly becomes a jealous and possessive lover and murders Juan. As the police investigate the murder, they suspect Pablo and the mysterious Laura P., whose letter has been found in Pablo's apartment. Distraught by his lover's death, the emotionally distressed Pablo has a car accident and suffers amnesia. In the meantime, Antonio has taken up with Tina as a way of getting closer to Pablo. When the police corner him, Antonio holds Tina hostage in her apartment, willing only to release her for an hour of passion with Pablo. Pablo agrees. After the hour, Antonio kills himself.

Despite such intricate narrative complexities, the central figures are all related to film and become part of a web of cinematic self-referentiality. At the center of that plot is Pablo's script of Tina's life. When she discovers that the script is about her, she rebukes her brother: "My problems with men are not just some plot for a movie script." Unfortunately, Tina's life has unraveled around her brother's film career and his deadly sexual liaison with Antonio who, in an effort to insinuate himself even further into Pablo's life, has seduced Tina. In this way, the film continually plays with the notion of movies vampirizing the lives of those who make them, blurring the lines between those lives and cinematic fiction.

The idea of recycling is the centerpiece of this cinematic self-reference. It is announced in the recycling of the letter authored by Pablo to be sent by Juan and Antonio's suggestion that Pablo write to him using the name Laura P. At the root of the film's plot and the recycling of Tina's life as film, however, lies the pattern of sexuality and family. As she recounts her autobiography to her amnesiac brother in an effort to trigger his memory, we learn that Tina was once Tino; he was seduced by their father and subsequently precipitated their parents' breakup. Tino went to Morocco with his father and, after a sex change, was abandoned by him. As Tina, she went to Paris and returned to Madrid only after her mother's death. In recounting her return to Madrid, Tina remarks as an aside, "Oh, by the way. This is Madrid." The gesture sums up the long process of transformation of the old Madrid into the cosmopolitan city reflected in the metamorphosed lives of its inhabitants.

Throughout *Law of Desire*, we see Tina, Pablo, and Ada, the daughter of Tina's lesbian lover (Bibi Andersen), posed as a newly reconstructed family that displaces the fractured one torn asunder by the complex sexual unions Tina has revealed. We come to view this new family as one created by a recycling of earlier sexual identities: a gay male as father; his sibling, now a lesbian transsexual, as mother; and the daughter of a lesbian to complete the new familial trinity. Sexual and social identity, according to the film, is comprised of recycled "old" identities. In this regard, the idea of recycling is not so much a gimmick to promote a sense of artistic creation as it is an affirmation of the new family. The traditional Spanish family, as noted in Almodóvar's earlier films, most recently in *What Have I Done to Deserve This?* is viewed as a form of confinement. The utopian project of Madrid is joined with the emergence of the new Spanish family.

It is also noteworthy that the treatment of gay characters breaks with most conventional representations of gays in Spanish or European cinema. There is no question of characters coming out of the closet. Tina and Pablo's Spain has been liberated by the culture of *La movida*. Characters no longer speak of sexual guilt or homophobia; and with the exception of Antonio, who in the early scenes is still repressed, there is no questioning of sexual mores or gay identity. Alberto Mira has argued that *Law of Desire* constitutes a dividing line of gay representations between Spain's transition to democracy and the "post-transition" (Mira, *De Sodoma* 561).

One of the most extraordinary aspects of the film, and certainly a major point for Spanish audiences, was Carmen Maura's tour-de-force rendition of a man transformed into a woman, a role whose emotional complexity dwarfs the essentially comic renditions of Dustin Hoffman's *Tootsie* or of Julie Andrews's *Victor/Victoria*. Unlike those protagonists, Maura is not given the luxury of camping up her role. She portrays a transsexual, not a cross-dresser, and therein lies the power of her performance. As Almodóvar explains: "[A]rtifice is her only truth; artifice, not lies: they're two very distinct things. Artifice is her only truth, and if the individual is not crazy, and the character Carmen plays is not, she knows herself to be artificial and she relishes with that imitation the essence of being a woman, the most intimate part of femininity. Carmen is required to imitate a woman, to savor the imitation, to be conscious of the kitsch part that there is in the imitation, completely renouncing parody but not humor" (López 53).

The theme of identity is relayed on the soundtrack through the persistent development of an aural dimension to the cinematic narrative that echoes the blurring of the lines of identity. We note this from the precredits, when two dubbers prompt a young man to enact a scene of autoeroticism. Their offscreen voices begin to suggest one of the central narrative motives of the film: the characters' coming to inhabit already constructed sexual identities. This theme is more fully dramatized as the words of Pablo's letter are read by four different voices: first Pablo as he writes it; then the child, Ada, as she reads it; then Juan as Pablo reads the letter he receives; and finally by Antonio as he picks up the letter. This ventriloquism dramatizes the way characters "occupy" the already constructed site of identity of another. This pattern intensifies and expands to include the central figure of Tina.

After the premiere of his latest film, *El paradigma del mejillón* (The Mussel's Paradigm), Pablo invites Tina to star in his production of the Jean Cocteau monologue "La voix humaine" (The Human Voice). The curious and inventive twenty-five-minute monologue consists of a woman speaking to her estranged lover over the telephone. Almodóvar describes it as "'the desperate cry of an abandoned woman'" (qtd. in Vidal, *El cine* 235), in which Cocteau's heroine parallels in dramatic intensity and circumstance Tina's situation with her own lover, Ada's mother. What is especially striking about the play is, as its title indicates, the insistence on the human voice. It thus functions to underscore the centrality of voice as a crystallization of the process whereby identities are (re)constructed. Almodóvar says that the monologue "'serves the same thematic function as the other songs in the film'" (qtd. in Vidal, *El cine* 235). He is referring to Jacques Brel's song, "Ne me quittes de pas" (Don't Leave Me), played as a recurrent reminder to Pablo of his loss of Juan and also recycled in his staging of "The Human Voice," now lip-synched by little Ada, and "Lo dudo" (I Doubt It), the Mexican *bolero* sung by Trío Los Panchos and lip-synched by Antonio and Pablo in the final sequence. One might also add the closing credit music, Bola de Nieve's "Déjame recordar" (Let Me Remember), a musical refrain of Tina's repeated lament that all she has are her bittersweet memories of failed love. The Cocteau play and the three songs suggest a transnational geography that includes Belgian, French, Mexican, and Cuban sounds, an identity that is subsumed within the figure of Tina, once again implying the transnational refiguring of a seemingly narrow Spanish identity.

Almodóvar refers to the use of the Cocteau dialogues and the song lyrics as *robos*—thefts or plagiarisms. The term is useful to understand the process of identity refiguration that is going on here, as it underscores one of the narrative and dramatic processes that will evolve throughout all of his films over the next decade. As Tina's role attests, identity appears to be less a matter of biological destiny than an active form of self-creation drawn from the mass media—songs, movies, and, in this film for the first time, theater. It is worth noting that the musical and theatrical source of that self-creation seems decidedly nostalgic. Just as the evocation of the post–Civil War song "La bien pagá" in *What Have I Done to Deserve This?* reveals an identity extracted from Spain's historical past, the musical identities in *Law of Desire* derive from an earlier era.

Even in the development of the urban mise-en-scène of Madrid, the sense of recycling the nostalgic past informs the film's construction. We see this in the evocation of the city under construction, particularly in the scaffolding that appears in the final sequences, suggesting, as Almodóvar notes, that "'Madrid is an old and experienced city, but full of life. Such seemingly endless cycles of deterioration and restoration represent the city's desire to live'" (qtd. in Vidal, *El cine* 205).

This process is perhaps most clearly evident in the film's elaborate final sequence. Antonio has been cornered by the police in Tina's apartment. He agrees to release her and a captured police detective in exchange for one hour with Pablo. Finally alone with his lover, Antonio puts on a phonograph record ("Lo dudo") that expresses the sentiments of pure, unfailing love, then proceeds to undress Pablo for their sexual union. The camera discreetly cuts away to a shot of the street below as the assembled police and relatives look up at the window.

After the lovemaking scene, Antonio, understanding that he is trapped, shoots himself in the head and falls dead before Tina's altar of kitsch artifacts—Barbie dolls and statues of Marilyn Monroe and the Virgin Mary. Pablo rushes to his side and, in a mock re-creation of Michelangelo's *Pietà*, holds his lover in his arms. The scene is thus constructed around an ironic inversion of Spanish institutional history.

Not only is a religious discourse mobilized to valorize gay sexual activities, but the dramatized audience, presumably the authenticators of that new demarginalization, are the police, the enforcers of repressive social and moral codes. In short, the apparatus of Francoist social and sexual repression is made to affirm the values that, historically, it blocked and suppressed.

With the international interest in Almodóvar and the press insistence that he was the "Spanish Fassbinder," occasioned by the film's explicit gay narrative, critics attempted to read the director's autobiography into the film (Smith, *Desire* 79–80; Vidal, *El cine* 194). To a certain degree, this crossover as gay cinema was teasingly played up by the Spanish press. *Fotogramas* ran a cover in October 1986 with the headline "Todos los Hermanos Eran Homosexuales" (All the Siblings Were Gay), referring not to Pedro and Agustín but rather Pablo and Tina. To Nuria Vidal, however, Almodóvar explained his particular understanding of the autobiographical connection to the film: "'In all of my films there are autobiographical elements, if by autobiographical we mean feelings more than anecdotes. If we speak of feelings, I'm in all my films, from the first to the last. If we also speak of plot elements, there are some recognizable [autobiographical] elements. But in all of them there are the things I love, the things I hate, the things I'm afraid of" (Vidal, *El cine* 195).

Law of Desire was Almodóvar's biggest box-office hit to date, winning a number of major international film awards, with the exception of two significant local ones: the Goya, given by the members of the Instituto de Cine, and the Spanish Association of Film Directors. The film is conspicuous as one of only two Almodóvar films (along with *Bad Educa tion* [2004]) to be completely snubbed by the Goyas. It has been widely conjectured that this was due to a generalized homophobic response among Spanish film critics and members of the film industry toward what amounted to the groundbreaking treatment of the normalization of gay romantic narratives in Spanish film (Mira, *De Sodoma* 560).

Women on the Verge of a Nervous Breakdown (1988)

Even before the Spanish premiere of *Law of Desire*, Almodóvar was busy developing the script for what would eventually become his most critically acclaimed film to date, *Mujeres al borde de un ataque de nervios* (Women on the Verge of a Nervous Breakdown). The budget was a relatively modest 130 million pesetas, three-quarters of which was supplied through government subventions (50 percent by the Ministry of Culture; 25 percent by State Television), and an additional portion by Lauren Films, which had been involved in producing and distributing *Law of Desire*. Despite financial restrictions, Almodóvar was able to begin an eight-week shoot exclusively in the Madrid area.

The original idea was to make an extremely low-budget affair that would star Carmen Maura in a variation of the staging of Cocteau's "Human Voice" sequence from *Law of Desire*. This staging was to be interrupted by a series of parodies of television commercials (Boquerini 98). The script grew through successive rewritings, however, as Almodóvar kept adding female characters to the cast until, as he himself noted, Cocteau had all but disappeared, and the film he now imagined was more like American comedies of the 1950s. Two essential features of the original conception remained, however: the feel of the film as a faux adaptation of a theatrical work (Strauss, *Conversaciones* 76), and the narrative situation in which the melodramatic heroine, Pepa (Carmen Maura), pursues every means possible to unburden her feelings to her estranged lover, Iván (Fernando Guillén). As in the Cocteau monologue, the heroine's male interlocutor is conspicuously absent throughout most of the film. The cast includes familiar faces from Almodóvar's troupe: Chus Lampreave, Antonio Banderas, Julieta Serrano, Kiti Manver, Rossy de Palma, and Ángel de Andrés.

Once again, at the root of Almodóvar's storytelling is an eclectic mix of images and elements that recall other films. The idea of narrative pastiche is introduced with the opening credit sequence, which shows a series of glossy magazine cutouts of female legs, an eye, female hands with painted red nails, and cutout images in successive frames of different parts of the female body. Besides underscoring one of the film's themes of women as mere objects to be collected by predatory males (Edwards 92), the collage emphasizes the creative process whereby Almodóvar regularly mounts his stories as a series of cultural objects positioned to tell a story.

In the opening narrative sequence, a second fast-cut collage of images introduces Pepa's penthouse apartment as she dreams of Iván's

Almodóvar and the cast of *Women on the Verge of a Nervous Breakdown.* Courtesy of El Deseo S.A.

philandering. This time, however, the collage style disorients the spectator, as elements of the story to be unfolded are presented without clear linkage. Almodóvar may be playfully mocking critics who had argued that he could not tell a coherent story, as he invites his audience to participate in deciphering images and sounds, a parallel to Pepa's ensuing search for Iván.

Even more self-referential than the collage is the way the film privileges a chain of image quotes from 1950s Hollywood comedies that, in effect, repositions Almodóvar's cinematic world closer to traditional Hollywood films. *Women on the Verge* may be read as a conscious effort at a cinematic crossover insofar as it conspicuously avoids sex and drugs, two elements that had restricted Almodóvar's previous films to alternative distribution markets. Their omission secures the seemingly wholesome effect of the Hollywood fifties style.

The plot details a two-day period in the life of Pepa, a professional movie dubber and television actress, and her lover, Iván, also a dubber, who has left a message on her answering machine that he is leaving her. Pepa needs to find Iván to inform him that she is pregnant with his child, but his womanizing makes him continually unavailable. Pepa and Iván have been hired to dub the voices of the two lead actors in Nicholas Ray's *Johnny Guitar,* but Pepa oversleeps and must voice her part without Iván, who is now off with his new lover, the feminist lawyer Paulina Morales (Kiti Manver). Pepa decides to purge her apartment of all memories of Iván, clearing out his belongings, burning the mattress they shared, and finally putting the apartment up for rent.

In short order, Iván's son Carlos (Antonio Banderas) and his fiancée, Marisa (Rossy de Palma), arrive to look at the apartment for a possible rental. When Carlos sees his father's picture in Pepa's bedroom, he becomes aware of their relationship. Carlos was born out of wedlock when his mother, Lucía (Julieta Serrano), was Iván's lover. When Iván abandoned Lucía, she went mad and was committed to a psychiatric hospital. She has recently been released and, like Pepa, is now in search of Iván; only Lucía is planning to murder him.

Pepa's solitude and melodramatic anguish are balanced by her cama-raderie with a variety of zany female characters, including Marisa and Candela (María Barranco), Pepa's friend who has been abandoned by her Shiite terrorist lover. After rapid-fire dialogue and fast-paced action, including a chase scene to the Madrid airport where Iván is about to depart with his new lover for Stockholm, the film ends on Pepa's terrace as Marisa awakens from a drug-induced sleep. She and Pepa "enjoy each other's company," as Peter W. Evans describes it, "at last temporarily released from the spell of sexual desire" (*Women* 9).

The story borrows much from Hollywood's neo-screwball comedies of the 1950s. Evans sees clear links to Jean Negulesco's *How to Marry a Millionaire* (1953), Billy Wilder's *The Apartment* (1960), and even Stanley Donen's musical *Funny Face* (1957). The apparent link to Donen's film relates to the mise-en-scène of Pepa's apartment, which imitates the uses of similar spaces in Hollywood's sophisticated screwball comedy: an elegant space with lavish colors (Allinson, *Spanish* 183). Despite the film's continual reference to specific streets and addresses, the Madrid of *Women on the Verge* is only a pastiche of a studio backdrop. In this idealized city, Almodóvar constructs an impossibly elegant Madrid sky-line to approximate that of New York, a ubiquitous part of the imagery of 1950s Hollywood comedies.

Evans argues persuasively that Hollywood melodrama of that same decade, especially Douglas Sirk's woman-centered works like *Magnificent Obsession* (1953), *All That Heaven Allows* (1954), and *Imitation of Life* (1958), inspired different aspects of the Carmen Maura–focused plot, mise-en-scène, and even color (*Women* 21). These intertextual elements again reflect the way Almodóvar appropriates Hollywood filmic style and integrates it into a specific Spanish context as part of a thematic refiguring of Spain's emerging modernity. The physical embodiment of the Transition is portrayed brilliantly by Carmen Maura. She defines an emotional trajectory that moves her from melodramatic excess—tossing telephones and phonograph records out the window, burning mattresses—to a state of self-confident repose in the final scene, suggesting her emotional growth and her entrance into modernity.

As presented in the film, Madrid embodies a vibrant Spanish cultural identity that rejects the traditions that ordered Spanish social life for four decades. One key element of this re-imaging is the depiction of women as freed from the mystification of patriarchal culture—fathers, lovers, and even sons—who have kept them in an inferior position. As Evans argues, "Ultimately, the film recognizes that masculinity is in crisis. . . . [M]asculinity is comically represented as also on the verge if not of a nervous breakdown then at least of structural fatigue, exposed as a construction formed by decades of a macho culture which affects and constrains the lives of men as well as of women" (*Women* 40).

Following the strategy of *Matador,* in which Vidor's *Duel in the Sun* became the cinematic core from which the Spanish plot derived its characters, *Women on the Verge* locates its dramatic center in the explicit Hollywood melodramatic intertext of the Joan Crawford/Sterling Hayden "Tell me lies" dialogue from Nicholas Ray's *Johnny Guitar* (1954). In the Ray film, Johnny (Sterling Hayden) tells Vienna (Joan Crawford): "Say something nice . . . lie. Say you've been waiting for me. . . . Say you love me too." Gwynne Edwards notes a certain irony in the way Vienna treats Johnny, which is the way that Pepa would like to treat Iván but cannot (94). As in many of Almodóvar's films, the cinematic self-reference also operates on a particularly Spanish metacinematic level, as it highlights the historical practice of Spanish distributors dubbing rather than subtitling foreign films. Pepa's job of dubbing Crawford's dialogue alludes to the desires of an audience that has grown comfortable with the falsification not only of voices but even of plot twists in Spanish films, as dubbing had been used to censor undesirable dialogue. It parallels an earlier scene in which Lucía's father tells her that she is lovely; she replies, "How well you lie, Papá. That's why I love you" (Evans, *Women* 44).

Celestino Deleyto explores the parodic texture of *Women on the Verge,* arguing that "[t]his is a film about voices, but not so much about real voices as about voices from films, not the voices of characters but the voices of actors. . . . Almodóvar's texts are about passion and desire but, in the films, these passions and desires are provoked by artifice, by other films, by actors" (55). Such a reading has far-reaching implications, not only for *Women on the Verge,* in which the self-referentiality of cinema is made explicit, but in later films such as *High Heels* (1991), *The Flower of My Secret* (1995), and *Talk to Her* (2002), in which an aural imagination becomes a determining factor in the formation and deformation of characters.

A number of plot complications have to do with the telephone as a theatrical prop involving the human voice. The action begins as Pepa is awakened by the voice of Iván on her answering machine, announcing that he is breaking off their relationship. These pieces of contemporary, everyday technology underscore the centrality of the human voice to the plot. Even the theme of predatory males who are responsible for the melodramatic state of the women of the title is rooted principally in the figure of Iván, who is more often heard than seen, yet whose presence is felt by nearly all the other principal characters. The gag of the phone and the answering machine, while essentially comic, underscores the central theme of the impossibility of communication.

As an antidote to Iván, the female voice is given prominence through a series of cinematic and musical intertexts that synthesize the heroine's almost theatrical solitude. These include the insertion of a television news program in which Almodóvar's mother, Francisca Caballero, reads the evening news in a monotone voice, and the presence of Candela, who, with her squeaky voice, even mocks the stutter of Carlos, Iván's son. The most conspicuous of all the emphases on the human voice is the cinematic self-references in the "Tell me lies" dialogue. In form and content, the lines spoken by Pepa's dubbing to the absent Iván, playing Johnny, acknowledges Iván's unfaithfulness outside the fiction and the power of his voice to deceive. That is, Vienna is aware that their love is a lie. Underscoring Iván's insincerity as a lover, Pepa is forced to record her lines in the dialogue alone.

Pepa's imposter-staging of Joan Crawford's voice is further echoed by two other female musical voices later in the film: those of Lola Beltrán singing the Mexican *ranchero* song "Soy infeliz" (I'm Unhappy), the melody of which is heard over the opening credits, and later that of the Cuban singer La Lupe's "Puro Teatro" (Play-acting), which accompanies the final credits. Almodóvar describes the two songs and their selection this way: "'Soy infeliz' is an old Mexican song that goes very well with the plot of the film: A woman who says she's unhappy because she's been abandoned. . . . There's another song with which the film ends that, curiously, is sung by La Lupe and is titled 'Puro Teatro.' In this case it's about a woman who tells her lover that he's been deceiving her with his play-acting, making an allusion to the hypocrisy of men. This song perfectly captures the film's ending" (Strauss, *Conversaciones* 77).

The use of Latin American popular songs, in obvious contrast to the possible inclusion of popular Spanish music, is significant for two reasons. First, in a film in which much of the geographic and cultural specificity of the Spanish milieu has been erased, the evocation of Latin American music anchors the emotional underside of the story within Hispanic cultural contexts with which the Spanish audience is familiar: Mexican *ranchero* music and Cuban music. Secondly, the musical "frame" of the film addresses the growing sense of a Hispanic transnational spectatorship that Almodóvar's cinema, through his brother Agustín's work, begins to cultivate in this period.

Ultimately, this alternative universe of female wisdom in the face of masculine fickleness and camaraderie among the women is posed as the theme of *Women on the Verge of a Nervous Breakdown*. As Almodóvar suggests, the film ends with the affirmation of a bond among women that seems to transcend the male world, a theme that goes back to the final sequence in *Pepi, Luci, Bom*, in which a similarly optimistic female bonding functions as narrative closure. As Núria Triana-Toribio suggests, that transcendence has developed out of a "recolonization" of the space once shared by Iván and Pepa in the apartment ("Almodóvar's" 185). The recolonization process involves disposing of all the familiar objects that bear the memory of her unfaithful lover: the mattress, suitcase, answering machine, and clothes. These are elements of what Triana-Toribio calls the "living mise-en-scène" (184).

Paul Julian Smith proposes a broader reading of the mise-en-scène of Pepa's penthouse apartment, as it embodies what he calls "a theory of contentment": "Its utopian thesis is that society has adapted itself to individuals, and all their social and professional needs have been met" (*Desire* 93). He goes on to note that the space of the terrace, which will be central to the film, unites country and city, upper and lower class, Spain and abroad. The skyline invoked is one that is simply impossible to see in Madrid. Rather, it operates as an abstract space of the comedic genre of "high comedy" (94). Modernity, embodied in the mediatized city within which Pepa and Iván move, carries vestiges of the old order, memorialized in the chicken coop Pepa keeps on her terrace and the traditional gazpacho she concocts.

Stuart Hall views the particular strategy of the film as a model for a hybridized European cinema that unself-consciously constructs an "authentic" European space: "This is a film which, by working scrupulously within its limits, most effectively breaks boundaries" (52). Positionality of cultural space is one of the critical elements of the film's construction of stories and characters. When Candela laments to Pepa, "Look what the Arab world has done to my life!" she echoes the self-awareness of the New Spain's position in relation to other cultures that had begun with the English-language lyrics from the credit sequence of *Pepi, Luci, Bom, and Other Girls on the Heap.*

Such positional self-awareness as it relates to the pursuit of a utopian milieu guides the formulation of *Women on the Verge* in other ways. Almodóvar has constructed a Madrid that acknowledges that the historical moment of *La movida* culture has passed and that Spaniards have normalized their place in a new geopolitical world. In this regard, the visual style of the film, most spectacularly the vibrant colors of the set and costumes (Allinson, *Spanish* 183), provides a fundamental revision of the imageability of Spain itself in European and world cinema. Madrid secures an image, at least within Almodóvar's films, as the locus of Spain's new modernity, viewed as sexy, cosmopolitan, and alluring. The price of that modernity, as Smith suggests, is the progressive loss of the psychic and social center: "Territorial space has become devalued" (*Vision* 44).

Women on the Verge of a Nervous Breakdown was the culmination of an extraordinary migration for the director from the margins of a marginalized national cinema to the gates of Hollywood, all within a period of eight years. Almodóvar's eighth commercial feature in as many years was nominated for an Oscar in the Best Foreign Film category. With effective international marketing through Orion Pictures, it went on to become one of the most commercially successful Spanish films of all time (Evans, *Women* 10). The impressive list of its awards includes Best Script from the 1988 Venice Film Festival; Best Foreign Film by the New York Film Critics' Circle; Best Film and Best Actress for Almodóvar and Maura at the 1989 Berlin Film Festival; five Goyas; and the Golden Globe for Best Foreign Film. Obviously, the most significant of these was the Oscar nomination for Best Foreign Film, even though it lost to Bille August's *Pelle, the Conqueror.*

Transnational Repositioning after *Women on the Verge*

Even without the prestige of an Oscar, *Women on the Verge of a Nervous Breakdown* earned Almodóvar the indisputable status of international auteur. In the films that follow, however, there is a conspicuous pulling back from the formula that gave him such wide popularity, what was dubbed by many Spanish commentators as "Almodóvar Lite." Drugs and sex returned as driving mechanisms of the plot of his next film, *¡Atame!* (Tie Me Up! Tie Me Down!; 1989), in which Victoria Abril plays an ex-junkie porn star whose partner, Antonio Banderas, is everything a Hollywood hero should not be, most notably, violent with women. In developing *Tie Me Up!* and the two films that followed, Almodóvar seemed to distance his work from Hollywood's models of middle-class morally defined cinema. It is no coincidence that, while playing Spanish patriarchy off of Hollywood genres (melodrama, screwball comedies, and film noir), these films do so in self-conscious ways that defy the unwritten code of Hollywood's mainstream moral formulation of characters and plots.

Tie Me Up! Tie Me Down! challenges the widely held conception abroad of Almodóvar as essentially a director of light comedies whose films merely lampoon aspects of contemporary Spanish society and culture, often with reckless abandon, rather than exploring serious themes.

Though there are moments of comedy in the films that follow, they rarely achieve the level of screwball comedy that runs from *Labyrinth of Passions* to *Women on the Verge* and had been one of the dominant features of his international reputation.

In 1991, Almodóvar entered into an arrangement with Ciby 2000, a mainstream French company, to coproduce what would eventually become four films: *High Heels, Kika, The Flower of My Secret,* and *Live Flesh.* Though he would contend that these are essentially Spanish films and that only the funding was French (Smith, *Desire* 177), Spanish cultural specificity is secondary in these works, often literally a mere backdrop to action. We see this in the painting of stylized flamenco dancers as the backdrop to Miguel Bosé's performance in *High Heels* and in the Andalusian set for Francisca Caballero's television show in *Kika,* "Hay que leer más" (You Have to Read More). Related to this evolution of mise-en-scène is a noticeable shift toward a negative characterization of Madrid, countering the image presented in his earlier films. In contrast to the bright and elegant mise-en-scène of *Matador* and *Women on the Verge,* the city in *Tie Me Up!* is reduced to images of drug dealers and street violence. One of the characters in *High Heels* announces, "Madrid is a dangerous city." Similarly, the setting of *Kika* is described by Mazierska and Rascaroli as "a hostile, frightening, unknowable metropolis" (37). With this change in tone comes an increased use of elaborate studio sets, often to simulate urban exteriors, an inevitable development, according to Almodóvar, given the increasing difficulty of shooting exteriors in Madrid (Mazierska and Rascaroli 37).

These elements contribute to a deeper change in the characters Almodóvar creates after *Women on the Verge.* He begins to focus on persons who are no longer easily recognized genre stereotypes, as in his previous films, but have a darker side that marks them as individuals. Paradoxically, they are characters formed and deformed by movie genres. Their drama is psychologically rooted in their own circumstances but is also symbolically a struggle against genre. In no small measure, the genre against which they rebel is the clichéd image of folkloric Spain recently cultivated as the director's calling card to international audiences. In this sense, in the five years following the triumph of *Women on the Verge,* Almodóvar continues to interrogate the shape and meaning of Spanish modernity.

Tie Me Up! Tie Me Down! (1989)

While working on *Women on the Verge of a Nervous Breakdown*, Almodóvar came up with an idea for a new film. He claims to have been motivated in part by the need for his next project to be a low-budget movie. Consequently, his plot would involve the same artificial set that had been one of the primary spaces of his previous film, Pepa's terrace apartment, now transposed into a movie-within-a-movie plot that emphasizes "the authenticity of artifice," as he called it (Almodóvar, *¡Atame!*). The core of the interplay between artifice and authenticity involves three characters who, like the backdrop that brings them together, are the products of cultural recycling. Marina Ozores, Max Espejo, and Ricky all derive their identities from movie genres. Each is further shaped by the way Max defines the genre of the film in which he is directing Marina: "un subproducto cultural" (a cultural subproduct). The aesthetic of Almodóvar's early films, with their kitsch recycling of popular culture, now takes a self-conscious turn, what in Spanish is called *desdoblamiento* (often translated as "interior duplication"), referring to the most common form of the baroque phenomenon, the play-within-the-play or movie-within-the-movie. But *desdoblamiento* may also mean the absorption of artifice in a character, as in Don Quixote's internalization of a fictional identity, or Unamuno's twentieth century existential novel *Niebla*, in which the protagonist, Augusto Pérez, discovers that he is merely a literary character and argues about his fate with his author, Unamuno. Almodóvar had been playing with such conceits since the creation of his literary alter ego Patty Diphusa and his later development of the melodramatic imagination in Pepa in *Women on the Verge*. This play of artifice, now taken as psychological and social reality, is a theme that, in one way or another, guides the development of this and the two films that follow.

The plot of *Tie Me Up! Tie Me Down!* focuses on Ricky (Antonio Banderas), who was orphaned at the age of three. As the film begins, he is released from a psychiatric hospital after twenty years of confinement. Ricky immediately pursues the former junkie and porn-movie queen, Marina Ozores (Victoria Abril), with whom he spent a night of torrid sex when he once escaped from his mental institution. He stalks Marina, sacking her dressing room at the movie studio, then breaks into her apartment where, as she resists, he bashes her with his head and breaks one of her teeth. Ricky then ties and binds her, a condition she must endure until, as he says, she falls in love with and marries him.

This story is paired with the plot of Marina's latest film—*El fantasma de medianoche* (Midnight Phantom), directed by the washed-up director Máximo Espejo (Francisco Rabal). *Midnight Phantom* appears to be a grade-B horror flick in the spirit of the original Don Siegal 1956 low-budget sci-fi film *Invasion of the Body Snatchers*, memorialized in a poster in the editing room. During her brief captivity, Marina is seen watching another horror film, George Romero's *Night of the Living Dead* (1968). Both films mirror Marina's double narrative: her bondage in drugs and by Ricky. At one point, Max Espejo observes that sometimes a love story can easily be confused with a horror story; indeed, Ricky has self-consciously shaped his life to conform to the model of a cinematic love story. From Marina's perspective, of course, it is more like a horror film. These films-within-the-film are joined by other movie quotes to create a self-referential cinematic texture. Principal among these are the stalker motif, a staple of horror films, and the inclusion of music from *Psycho* as a Hitchcock homage that mirrors Ricky's stalking and brutalization of Marina.

The premise of the plot and the central character of Ricky are rooted in this mediatized notion of personal identity in the age of mechanical reproduction, specifically, popular Hollywood-style movie plots: Boy meets girl, boy gets girl. After his release from the psychiatric hospital, Ricky's goal is to imitate a certain obvious cinematic model of that normalcy. At one point during Marina's captivity, he declares his intentions to her: "I'm twenty-three years old. I have fifty thousand pesetas, and I'm alone in the world. I would like to be a good husband to you and a good father to your children." The affirmation seems at first comical in its simplicity, but Ricky obstinately follows his script until, at last, Marina succumbs to his plot. He has accepted versions of the socialized conventions of love and marriage as the course of his life that have been mediated through popular culture. Ricky is the author of his own identity in the same way that Don Quixote is. He has willed his own destiny, but Almodóvar makes clear that it is a destiny shaped by a suspect set of mass-media-constructed fantasies.

Through these movie-identified characters and the kitsch films that define them, *Tie Me Up! Tie Me Down!* flaunts its popular, low-culture

Almodóvar directing Victoria Abril
in a scene from *Tie Me Up! Tie Me Down!*
Courtesy of the Filmoteca Española.

genealogy. In Ricky, Almodóvar has created a truly marginal character—the orphan from a rural village turned into a psychologically dis-
oriented thief and stalker. In Marina, the combination of drugs and
pornography situates her within the culture of vulgar, popular tastes,
which is underscored by the décor of her apartment.

In no small measure, the flaunting of popular tastes comes through
Almodóvar's development and exploitation of Victoria Abril's screen
persona. Abril's professional relationship with Almodóvar goes back
to *What Have I Done to Deserve This?* when he offered her the role
of Cristal. She turned it down, in part, she said, because it cast her in
the stereotype of the prostitute. She did, however, make an uncredited
cameo appearance at the beginning of *Law of Desire*. By 1989, when
Abril starred in *Tie Me Up!* she already had a well-established screen
persona. The thirty-year-old actress had appeared in fifty motion pictures, securing a reputation for powerful dramatic performances but
also for portrayals of female characters with strong sexual identities,
often of a humble or marginal social class.

Her sexual persona becomes one of the driving forces of the narrative. Not only is Abril cast as a former porn star, but she also appears nude in several scenes that emphasize her identification as a sexual object. The combination of these nude scenes, Ricky's physical assault on Marina, and her eventual defense of his actions provoked critical ire from feminists outside of Spain. In a revealing comment on her work with Almodóvar, Abril observed: "Pedro told me that he didn't want a female 'type'; what he wanted was for me to be me. . . . It was hard, because what I really like is to be someone else, to move out of myself" (qtd. in Álvarez and Frías 300). Instead of encouraging a method-actor approach to her character, Almodóvar coached Abril to play Marina as the recycled Abril persona, a sexualized movie star.

As part of the earthy popular-culture vein that Almodóvar taps into in the development of his protagonists, he joins cinematic self-reference with a depiction of kitsch religious iconography. Although such treatment of religious icons and rituals runs through his early films, from *Dark Habits* through *Law of Desire,* it becomes one of the pivots of the visual and thematic structure of *Tie Me Up!* in ways that distinguish this film from its predecessors. Almodóvar aligns his protagonists with a series of Catholic religious icons that recall the popularized religious art that was an integral part of national-Catholic culture in the post–Civil War period. These images are not high art, by any means. Rather, as Alejandro Yarza contends, they were pedagogical tools at the service of the arbiters of Catholic education (124). Thus, they introduce a curious hint of nostalgia that will eventually resurface with the return to the rural village of Ricky's early childhood in the film's final sequence.

Kitsch images of the Sacred Heart of Jesus and the Virgin Mary are introduced in the credit sequence. The film's titles are projected against an extreme close-up of the classical representation of the Sacred Heart of Jesus. As the camera gradually pulls back, we see that this is one of a series of three identical copies of the figure of Jesus aligned horizontally, below which is a row of identical images of the Virgin Mary. Yarza notes that the depiction shows Jesus and Mary at nearly the same age, as if to prefigure a similar pairing of Ricky and Marina. The offscreen sound that accompanies these images is that of a heartbeat made more pronounced as the camera recedes. As the screen finally is filled with the six pictures of Jesus and Mary, accompanied by the prominent sound of the heartbeat, the total image has the effect of a Warholesque silk-screen. The heartbeat depletes the image of any sacred meaning by literalizing the religious symbol, transforming it into a human heart. In Ricky's first act upon release from the hospital, he purchases a heart-shaped box of chocolates for Marina, thus concluding the process, as we see the transformation of the human heart to its socially constructed consumerist usage. The image of the box of chocolates that he gives to Marina reflects Ricky's metaphoric "giving of his heart" to the woman he loves.

Paul Julian Smith contends that the conceptual and emotional work in the film is carried out by the image itself and not the plot (*Laws* 205). In fact, the images work in tandem with the plot to underscore the process whereby distinctions between images and the world they represent are weakened, leading in this instance to Ricky's acceptance of the Hollywood plotting of his life. The point is underscored later in the film when Ricky and Marina watch a commercial for a German insurance company that mocks the Spaniards' lack of foresight and planning. At the end of the commercial, as if motivated by what she has just seen, Marina asks Ricky about his plans for the future. He replies by mimicking a Hollywood plotline: "To marry you and have your children."

Describing the way the religious motif is worked into the film's narrative logic, Martha J. Nandorfy notes the identification of Marina with the Virgin Mary: "Even though she is subjected to [Ricky's] authority, his story demands that she hold the keys to his salvation, like the mother of God" (55). Later, when Ricky returns to the apartment bloodied after a mugging by a drug pusher, Marina is moved to tears. Nandorfy again notes the religious cast to the scene: "[She] completely assumes the identification of the Mater Dolorosa; the image of her cleansing his wounds while crying, duplicating the Christian iconography of the painting over the bed" (58). Marsha Kinder notes Almodóvar's reworking of the Oedipal narrative, with Marina "finally being turned on by the Christlike wounds of her amorous orphaned kidnapper" (*Blood* 225).

Such self-conscious alignment of characters with Catholic iconography is apparently aimed at disengaging the spectator from the narrative, just as Marina submits to Ricky as the embodiment of a traditional patriarchal narrative. While in traditionalist Spain religious iconography might have served to seduce individuals to social roles, here the process of submission is disrupted by being transformed into a kitsch *tableau vivant*. Like the staging of the television spot, it creates a Brechtian kind of distance from the film that makes visible the patterns of social deformation of individuals through the endless repetition of mass-cultural images and icons (Yarza 129).

The film's presumed "happy ending," through which the narrative reaches closure by uniting Ricky with Marina, has been read variously as a subversively ironic trope. Ricky's return to his native village in Extremadura marks Almodóvar's first important break from the urban milieu of his previous films. In the final moments, not only has Marina accepted Ricky, but he appears also to have accepted his place in what will be a reconstituted family of only women. The status of women in a position of power is affirmed by the fact that Marina drives the car in the closing scene. As her sister Lola (Lolés León) and Ricky sing along with a cassette recording of the song "Resistiré" (I Will Survive), Marina remains silent, smiling, her eyes swelling with tears. Smith calls this moment "a double miming" in which Almodóvar accepts "the continuing survival of the heterosexual narrative (boy meets girl) in a radically relativized form" (*Laws* 211). Yarza contends that the characters singing along to "Resistiré" is a mark of Marina's continued resistance to the patriarchal ideology of the family from *within* the family.

Such ambiguous readings relate to one of the most powerful aspects of the film: the tour-de-force acting by Antonio Banderas. Perhaps inadvertently, Almodóvar takes a generic character—the stalker-voyeur—and gives him emotional depth. Ricky transcends the stereotype and is so completely humanized that Marina—and the audience—eventually succumb to his charms. This curious moral slippery slope will be repeated nearly fourteen years later in *Talk to Her*, where moral judgment about the rape of a comatose hospital patient is somehow suspended by audiences in an affective response to the rapist.

The international reaction to the film was far less subtle and nuanced. Reviews in the mainstream Spanish press were strongly positive. It came largely as a surprise, therefore, when the film and its director met hostility first in the press conference followings the screening at the Berlin Film Festival (Leavitt 36) and then in the events surrounding its U.S. release. Oddly enough, as Almodóvar later noted, the sexuality of *Law of Desire* was more explicit than that of *Tie Me Up! Tie Me Down!* but questions were raised about the bathing scene, the lovemaking scene between Banderas and Abril, and even the scene in which Abril urinates. Most of all, German, British, and American critics were appalled by Banderas's brutalization of Abril and her later defense of his actions.

Prior to its U.S. distribution, the film received an X rating from the Motion Picture Association of America (MPAA), which effectively disqualified it for general distribution. Indignant at the classification and defiant at what he saw as a variation of the kind of censorship tactics used under the Franco regime, Almodóvar and his U.S. distributor, Miramax, sued the MPAA. This was to be the first of a series of fights over the next five years with what Almodóvar saw as the American morality police. Miramax and Almodóvar eventually prevailed, and a new category, NC-17, was designed that reflected more appropriately the film's mature subject matter.

Almodóvar was able to turn this minor classification scandal to his advantage by refusing to play by the rules imposed by Jack Valenti and the MPAA. In the weeks that followed the Miramax suit, his name continually appeared in the international press, not as entertainment but as news. He was thus able to shape his expanding public persona from merely an entertaining and outspoken director of offbeat comedies to a bona fide defender of free expression. At the height of the scandal, he wrote an op-ed piece for *El País* entitled "Industry and Hypocrisy" in which he charged that the MPAA's classification system masks "the same Kafkian sensation of dark intransigence" that thirty years earlier characterized the Franco regime's approach to film censorship through classifications ("Industria"). He argued that such a classification system effectively transforms filmmakers into self-censors, as was the case under the dictatorship. His passionate defense ultimately strengthened the aura of Almodóvar's newly achieved identity as a transnational film author.

High Heels (1991)

At the end of *Tie Me Up! Tie Me Down!* Ricky returns to his native village, a place in the past that no longer exists. The village has long since been abandoned, his house left in ruins. There remains for Ricky only a treasured photo of his parents in front of the house. Almodóvar begins his next film, *Tacones lejanos* (High Heels), with an analogous scene in which Rebecca (Victoria Abril) waits at an airport to be reunited with her mother and similarly recalls painful scenes of childhood separation. The theme of revisiting the past, introduced at the end of the previous film, becomes an essential narrative axis in *High Heels*.

When he completed the shooting of *Tie Me Up! Tie Me Down!* Almodóvar had planned to make a short about a television news anchor who announces a murder on her program, then confesses to it onscreen, giving details of the crime. She explains that, even after killing the man, her husband, she still loves him, and then displays photographs of mementos of their life together that she retrieved after the murder. As Almodóvar explains, "If not for the second part of the scene, the confession would be just a gag, a quick comic rather than dramatic effect. This way, it turns into something disturbing" (*Tacones*). With his inimitable talent for creating complex plots from simple, comic situations, he went on to construct the elaborate narrative of *High Heels*.

This was El Deseo's first international coproduction with Ciby 2000, a mainstream French production company that, despite Almodóvar's status as an alternative cultural figure, saw the opportunity to market his films profitably in Europe. Almodóvar wrote *High Heels* with Antonio Banderas in mind, again pairing the *malagueño* actor with Victoria Abril as an "odd couple." The script called for Banderas's character to play multiple roles, one of which was to be a cross-dressing nightclub impersonator of Abril's fictional mother.

The plot, which Almodóvar calls a "tough melodrama," centers not on the newsreader but on her mother, Becky del Páramo (Marisa Paredes), a famous torch singer of the late 1960s who returns to Madrid after a fifteen-year absence. As Rebecca waits for her at the airport, the grown daughter relives through flashback key moments of her childhood animosity against her stepfather, whose death the young Rebecca engineered. Since childhood, her love-hate relationship with her mother has led her to imitate Becky in dress and manner, even as she has guarded a rancor toward Becky for having abandoned her to her natural father (Nacho Martínez) in order to pursue her musical career in Mexico. Rebecca's imitation of Becky leads her to marry her mother's former lover, Manuel (Feodor Atkine), the owner of a private television station that now employs Rebecca as a news anchor.

When Manuel seeks to rekindle an affair with Becky, his former lover, she realizes that her daughter's marriage is a failure. Manuel is found murdered in his chalet, and mother and daughter become prime suspects. The district attorney, Eduardo Domínguez (Miguel Bosé), is called to investigate the case. By night Domínguez works undercover trying to solve a murder at the Club Villarosa, where he performs as a female impersonator of Becky del Páramo, lip-synching Becky's old torch songs under the stage name Femme Letal. Rebecca does not recognize Domínguez as Femme Letal, with whom she made love backstage at the Villarosa and whose child she is now carrying. Rebecca confesses to Manuel's murder on her news show and is placed in jail the same day that Becky performs in her heralded return to the Spanish stage. Domínguez is not convinced of Rebecca's guilt. Rebecca did in fact kill her husband, just as she had earlier been the cause of her stepfather's death. The film ends with Becky sacrificing herself for her daughter, falsely confessing to the murder and faking the appropriate evidence for Domínguez.

The central dramatic focus of *High Heels* is the mirroring of identities of mother and daughter. Moving beyond the formulation of this theme around plotting, Marsha Kinder identifies a second duplicative element in what she calls the "audio fetish" in the film, in which mother and daughter have professions in which voice is central ("Matricide" 149). The emphasis on Rebecca's voice is comically conveyed through the onscreen presence of Isabel (Miriam Díaz Aroca) signing Rebecca's news reports for deaf audiences as her mother watches on television. Later, the presentation of Becky's singing voice in the *bolero* "Piensa en mí" (Think of Me) for her stage return reverses the pattern and shows Rebecca as the addressee of Becky's songs. As Kinder notes, the aural fetish eventually becomes the agency through which the film's narrative undermines patriarchal control over women.

The dramatic tension between Becky and Rebecca, reflecting the affection for and disavowal of genealogy and history, is deliberately constructed to evoke the audience's memory of a series of mother-daughter plots from famous Hollywood melodramas such as *Mildred Pierce, Stella Dallas*, and *Imitation of Life*. Rebecca even self-consciously refers to Ingmar Bergman's *Autumn Sonata* when she dramatically clashes with her mother. For David Thompson, such references suggest an awkward narrative scenario that simply invokes and imitates plots from other films, revealing "Almodóvar's characters' inability to achieve their own sense of identity outside a world of devoted reference" (62). As with his earlier films, critics outside of Spain, largely ignorant of Spanish cultural history, have tended to dismiss or, as in Thompson's case, to misread the ways in which Almodóvar employs Hollywood genre quotes "to articulate a position on the margins of Spanish society, one which calls into question the naturalness of categories of class and gender, as caught within the cinematic crossfire, as it were, of differing sociohistorical contexts" (Vernon, "Scripting" 325).

We see this, for example, in the way family genealogy is used as one of the organizing principles of *High Heels*. The mother-daughter tensions detailed from the first postcredit flashback finally are resolved at film's end in the Madrid basement apartment where Becky grew up. With a picture of her parents on the nearby wall, Becky dies in bed. Sobbing, the pregnant Rebecca climbs onto her mother's body and curls up in a fetal position. Pointedly, four generations of the Spanish family are evoked in the final image of the film. Almodóvar mines the idea of genealogies not only as personal identities but also as the historical-cultural genealogy of post-Franco Spain. Kinder notes, for instance, the choice of Miguel Bosé, the son of the famous Spanish matador Luis Miguel Domínguin and the Italian film actress Lucía Bosé. This makes for a subliminal plot element within which patterns of Spanish cultural identity are seen as hybridizing a presumably "pure" Spanish culture of Francoist ideology.

This kind of genealogical detail helps to bring into focus the broader historical structure of the film. Becky's return to Spain after the dismantlement of Francoism is the occasion for characters and audience to acknowledge their distance from the recent past. As in Ricky's remembrance of a rural Spain now lost, *High Heels* poses a similar evocation of the past through its play on recent historical icons and images. Most conspicuously, we see this in the brilliant staging of Femme Letal's performance at the Villarosa at which Becky and Rebecca are present. Not only is Letal's performance a fossilized depiction of Becky's look and style before she left Spain in the early 1970s, but, as Teresa Vilarós points out, the musical number, "Recordarás" (You Will Remember), invokes personal and collective history (218–19). The backdrop against which Letal performs is an incongruous tableau of traditional Andalusian models of femininity. The drag impersonation, however, also constitutes a frozen-in-the-past figure, since it portrays the Becky of a previous decade. The real Becky is, in effect, a spectator of herself. But with her daughter at her side, she is seeing her future as well. As Vilarós persuasively argues, the scene proposes the contemporary rewriting of oppressive patriarchal, Francoist culture. Tellingly, at this juncture spectators see a subversion of gender and a mark of the culture of endless duplication, imitation, and refraction whereby the original is distorted and then consumed as performance. To add to the vertiginous quality of the scene, as Letal performs for Becky and Rebecca, across the room is a row of cross-dressers, apparently Letal's groupies, who imitate her every gesture.

Though the emotional center of *High Heels* is the melodramatic relation of mother and daughter, the conceptual center of the film for Almodóvar appears to be the character of Femme Letal. Eduardo Domínguez keeps changing—he is a female impersonator, an undercover agent named Hugo, Inspector Domínguez, son to his mother, and finally, the father of Rebecca's baby. He comes to embody the fluidity of social relations and, more importantly, of gender, just as the film appears to flow from melodrama to thriller to Almodóvarian comedy. Although Almodóvar originally wrote the role of Femme Letal for Antonio Banderas, Miguel Bosé makes a unique personal contribution that may fit even better than Banderas's talents in that he is able to play off his real-life celebrity persona. In his own film and music career, Bosé has often capitalized on his androgynous features, the most notable of which is his facial resemblance to his actress mother. Letal's multiple identities underscore the essential hybridity of the cultural moment in which the patterns of patriarchal society, embodied in the predatory Manuel, are in the process of being eliminated (the murder plot) or made over through parody (Femme Letal and her groupies). Early in the film, Becky explains to her daughter that Margarita, her secretary, is writing Becky's autobiography. Beyond the gag point of the line, Becky enunciates one of the key points of the transformation of Spanish culture of the nineties to which earlier Almodóvar films only allude: authorial identity is rooted in the individual's assumption of already constructed identities and roles, now reinvested with new cultural meanings.

While the commercial response to *High Heels* was strong in Spain, it was considerably more muted than with *Women on the Verge* or even

Tie Me Up! Tie Me Down! It has come to be seen as one of Almodóvar's minor films. Yet it is through his fortuitous scripting and casting of the character of Becky del Páramo that Almodóvar "rediscovers" Marisa Paredes. Her tour-de-force performance would lead to their astounding collaboration in *The Flower of My Secret* and *All about My Mother.* Paredes had only been a secondary character in *Dark Habits* (Sister Manure); in *High Heels* she begins to appear as the heir to Carmen Maura's legacy as Almodóvar's new melodramatic heroine.

Kika (1993)

With *Kika,* Spanish critics joined the international chorus of negative reviews of Almodóvar's recent films. The complex narrative discontinuities in particular led many to view Almodóvar's tenth feature film as utterly incoherent. Like *High Heels, Kika* was conceived as a coproduction with Ciby 2000 and Canal+, a private Spanish television network partly owned by French interests. By the early nineties, of Spanish filmmakers, only Bigas Luna, whose recent *Jamón Jamón* (1992) had been a resounding European and international hit, could boast of such a solid financial and artistic positioning. *Kika's* poor critical reception outside Spain, however, seemed to confirm the widely held view in film circles that such international coproductions were doomed to be mere "Europuddings." Their only reason for being was to tap into the European Union's euphoric promotion of a transnational European cinema.

The plot opposes the sick urban space of Madrid with an idealized rustic space, Casa Youcalli. The urban space is concentrated in the apartment building where Ramón (Alex Casanovas), a morose fashion photographer, lives with his girlfriend Kika (Verónica Forqué), an airy and optimistic beautician who saved his life after an attack of narcolepsy. Casa Youcalli is an inheritance from his mother that Ramón shares with his stepfather, Nicolás Pierce (Peter Coyote), an American writer of pulp fiction. Unbeknownst to Ramón, Nicolás has had occasional sexual encounters with Kika.

Amidst a series of flashbacks that clumsily fill in the various complexities of these relations, the central plot comes into focus around Kika's rape by a porn star and prison escapee, Paul Bazzo (Santiago Lajusticia), who is the brother of Kika's lesbian maid, Juana (Rossy de Palma). The rape scene is videotaped by Ramón and passed on to Andrea

Caracortada (Victoria Abril), the hostess of the grotesque reality show "Lo peor del día" (The Worst of the Day). When Andrea shows up at Kika's apartment to get footage for her show, Kika refuses to speak to her. Eventually, the rape video is aired, and when Kika discovers that Ramón was responsible for the videotaping, she leaves him.

Andrea pieces together details of the video and aspects of Nicolás's latest manuscript to conclude that he is a serial killer who has transformed his deadly activities into the subject matter of his novels. She goes to Youcalli to confront him. Ramón had earlier concluded that Nicolás killed his mother. Andrea and Nicolás die in a shoot-out, and Kika runs off to the south with a hitchhiker.

Almodóvar describes *Kika* as "'a film about the sickness of big cities'" (qtd. in Strauss, *Un cine* 126), a theme that largely emerges by way of contrast with the idealized Casa Youcalli. Introduced first in a flashback, the house is the nostalgic space of Ramón's identification with his mother. As Almodóvar later explains, it is the "place of the illusion of happiness." Taken from a song by Kurt Weil, the vision of Youcalli is, according to Weil's lyrics, "the land of my desires, / Youcalli is happiness, pleasure. / But it's just a dream, a caprice, / Youcalli does not exist" (Strauss, *Conversaciones* 103).

Juxtaposed against this bucolic ideal is the apartment inhabited by Ramón and Kika. When Nicolás needs a place to stay upon returning to Madrid, he accepts their upstairs loft, where his actions are indirectly overheard from Ramón's apartment below. The framing of certain scenes suggests a panoptic mise-en-scène in which the characters are viewed from an offscreen location. The cityscape has been replaced by a dehumanized mediascape populated by all-seeing photographic cameras, television monitors, and the off-site video camera, all of which appear to cater to the insatiable voyeuristic impulse of the city's inhabitants. Indeed, the rape scene demonstrates an intimate connection between violence and voyeurism. In this stylized postmodern space, various technologies intrude upon the lives of the characters and then recirculate as images that will take over their lives. Mazierska and Rascaroli assert that "[t]he idea of the urban apartment as a semi-transparent space through which we look and are looked at, and in which we find no privacy or protection from external (or internal) aggression, is fundamental in the film, and is strengthened by a constant framing of the characters not only through windows, but also through frames of all types, as the circular skyline in Ramón and Kika's kitchen door" (38).

The film's intricate plot places Kika at the center of the action, even though Verónica Forqué was considerably less well known than Victoria Abril, who had recently starred in Vicente Aranda's international hit *Amantes* (Lovers; 1990). Speaking of the character of Kika in relation to his conception of the film, Almodóvar explains: "The world that surrounded me and my own world were threatening to asphyxiate me. I needed a good dose of optimism. I wanted to recover the fresh air of a comedy both for my films and for myself. That was how the genesis of *Kika* the title and Kika the character came about. An innocent girl, like the best of Marilyn [Monroe], who has no sense of the risks in life (like Candela in *Mujeres*), optimistic and without prejudices, always ready (like Patty Diphusa), who's sensitive and contemporary (like Holly Golightly from *Breakfast at Tiffany's,* my eternal point of reference). A character with an almost surreal optimism" ("Génesis" 11).

Against the metacinematically inspired figure of Kika comes a series of characters who are seen as foils to her naturalness and upbeat personality. As Almodóvar says, each is identified with a particular genre: Andrea Caracortada (television/reality shows); Nicolás Pierce (novels/thrillers); Ramón (fashion photography). In particular, the Victoria Abril character was intended to be a kind of opposition figure to Kika: the pessimist to Forqué's cockeyed optimist. In their two previous collaborations, Almodóvar played against Abril's established film persona, her powerful dramatic skills, and her sexual persona. Trapped in the Jean-Paul Gaultier spacesuit that Andrea Caracortada wears to film the day's tragedies, however, she seems more cyborg than sexual being. Paul Julian Smith goes even further in posing the contrast in ways that reflect upon the polarity of the spaces as two essentially false constructions of the feminine: "In *Kika* gender is technologized, with the 'essential' woman dissolved into visual paraphernalia (false eyelashes and fun fur), then in Andrea technology is gendered . . . revealed to be not simply instrumental but rather complicit with the powers of patriarchy, even as it is embodied in a figure empirically gendered feminine" (*Vision* 49–50).

The intricate plot of *Kika* revolves around a pivotal theme that has been at the heart of Almodóvar's films beginning explicitly with *Tie Me*

Up! Tie Me Down!: the blurring of the lines between life and its mediated representations. As early as *Pepi, Luci, Bom,* Carmen Maura explains to her friends whose autobiographies she wants to videotape that it is essential to perform, to "act" one's life for the camera, otherwise it will not seem real. With Ricky in *Tie Me Up!* the problem becomes the centerpiece of the plot: the hero has internalized the fiction of movies to shape the design of his life. In *Kika,* from the opening credits, in which Ramón shoots close-ups of the face of his fashion model as if in orgasmic ecstasy, we see the image of the male employing photographic technology to simulate the sexual act. Borrowed from a famous sequence in Michelangelo Antonioni's *Blow-Up,* the scene suggests the complex derivative discourses that shape Ramón's sense of his own sexual identity. We later discover that he needs to repeat this technologized simulation of copulation to excite himself in bed with Kika.

This is the same bed on which Kika will be raped by Paul Bazzo, the porn star, as the couple is being videotaped by Ramón from a nearby studio. Almodóvar's objective in the grotesque scene, which claims over ten minutes of screen time, is in part to underscore similarities between the porn star and the photographer. As Susan Martin-Márquez notes: "Bazzo [is] incapable of distinguishing fiction from reality and furthermore . . . models his real-life criminal actions on the imaginary world of cinema. When he rapes the female protagonist, Kika, at knifepoint, his victim begs him to put down his weapons, but Paul refuses asserting that '*así se ve mejor. En los rodajes siempre lo decían*' (it looks better that way. They always said so on the set)" (29). Bazzo is thus a character whose outlook is, like Ramón's, contaminated by mediatized representations taken as life. He is also the logical extension of the confusion between representation and personal belief earlier dramatized in Banderas's Ricky and, to a lesser degree, the same symptomatic conflation of mediatized and personal identity embodied by Rebecca in *High Heels.*

This double bind of mediated perception is at the heart of the setup, as the rape sequence is viewed in breakaway shots from the perspective of Ramón's video camera. Andrea's acquisition of the videotape will cause the rape scene to be relived as television fare on her reality show, thus implicating other audiences—the television audience, Kika and Ramón as they sit in their living room, and ultimately the film's real audience—in viewing the rape through a voyeur's perspective. Almodóvar describes the scene as consisting of two rapes: "One is the physical one, and the other takes place through the communications media—which is what the film is about" (Troyano 102).

Characters like Ramón and Bazzo appear as symptomatic products of a society technologized and mediatized for the raw consumption of sexuality to such a degree that they are otherwise impotent, as in the case of Ramón, or sexually deranged, as in the case of Bazzo. The emblematic figure of that deformation, however, is Andrea Caracortada. Her Gaultier costume technologizes her, depriving her of humanity or even, as the figure of Abril is recognized, of any sexual allure. The character of Andrea is, tellingly, scarred and deformed, her exposed breast and the scar on her face recalling the ways in which sexual attractiveness has been mutilated by the mechanized, commercialized media.

One of the themes that may be obscured by the complexity of the film's intricate plot is the crisis of artistic creation. The two creative figures in the film, Ramón and Nicolás, have each devised a form of creativity based on recycling. For Ramón, it is a question of personal sexual gratification that folds back upon his relation with his mother, treated so self-consciously in the plot as to be a parody of Oedipal desire. For Nicolás, creativity consists of recycling life into art, killing women and then transforming the story of their murder into best sellers. In both cases, the concept of creativity within the postmodern world evoked by the city is put into crisis that shows no signs of solution.

One of the seminal sources of Almodóvar's films since *Women on the Verge of a Nervous Breakdown* has been Hitchcock's *Rear Window*, appropriately translated into Spanish as *La ventana indiscreta* (The Indiscreet Window). It is the indiscretion of a community deformed by an illusory sense of modernity that has been buttressed by dehumanizing technology. Even as the film emphasizes certain recognizable cityscapes, it depicts a city largely devoid of human affect. As Smith says: "Now territorial space has been devalued (now Kika has no home to return to), we are lost in the vision machine with Almodóvar; and we may, like his heroine, feel we have lost our way" (*Vision* 44).

The problems of *Kika*'s hostile critical reception were compounded by new censorship difficulties in the United States. The film received a restrictive classification, NC-17, the category created by the MPAA in response to Almodóvar's protests about *Tie Me Up! Tie Me Down!* The *New York Times* censored one of the ads for the film that showed Victoria Abril's exposed breast. Despite Almodóvar's passionate defense of *Kika* to the media, it appeared that, like his characters, he had also reached a creative impasse from which he needed to stand back and reassess his career and creative direction. That reassessment would come by way of his next film, *La flor de mi secreto* (The Flower of My Secret), in many respects developed as a creative autobiography.

The Flower of My Secret (1995)

La flor de mi secreto (The Flower of My Secret) signals a new period of creative energy in Almodóvar's cinema. It was the first of his films since *Women on the Verge* to enjoy resounding critical acclaim, in Spain and elsewhere, as he appeared to have returned to a style of filmmaking that pleased him as well as his audiences. For a number of textual as well as contextual reasons, the film marks a change in Almodóvar's recent development. *The Flower of My Secret* has none of the heavy sex scenes of the previous three films, perhaps a tacit concession to the strong criticisms of feminists and the MPAA. Less well noted, however, is the change in tone and authorial outlook from the cynicism of *Kika*. Almodóvar himself notes that, unlike the films that precede it, there are no bad people in *The Flower of My Secret* (Almodóvar, *La Flor*). The values and emotions of the characters in his eleventh film seem to embrace an optimistic worldview despite many outwardly negative themes, such as marital infidelity, attempted suicide, and drug addiction, all of which punctuate the story.

The plot focuses on Leocadia Macías (Marisa Paredes), a writer caught in a variety of personal and professional crises. The most prominent professional crisis is her rejection of her successful career as the author of best-selling romance novels (*novelas rosa*) that she writes under the pen name Amanda Gris. Leo is dissatisfied with the superficiality of the genre in which she is trapped by contract. In an effort to help, her friend Betty (Carmen Elías) introduces Leo to Ángel (Juan Echanove), the literary editor of *El País*. Not realizing that she is the author of the Amanda Gris novels, Ángel hires Leo to write critiques of her own novels under a new pseudonym, Paz Sufrategui.

Leo's dissatisfaction with her literary activity is rooted in despondency over her failed marriage to Paco (Imanol Arias) and the difficult time her mother (Chus Lampreave) is having living with Leo's sister, Rosa (Rossy de Palma), in a working-class suburb of Madrid. These crises are joined in the key sequence of the film in which Paco walks out on Leo and her subsequent attempted suicide is thwarted by a phone call from her mother. Leo returns with her mother to their native village. Before departing, she learns that Betty was having an affair with Paco but has broken it off because of the way he has treated Leo.

With the support of her mother, Leo is able to revive her spirit and regain her energies. Moving to the village helps her set in perspective the failure of her marriage and her disillusionment with her writing career. The shift of setting makes clear that the city she left behind mirrors her emotional state. Leo's disaffection from the city, however, derives not simply from a sociological situation that intrudes upon action and character from beyond the script, as it had in *Kika;* it comes from the heroine's own emotional state. Almodóvar has at last found the dramatically plausible situation that makes disaffection from the city a symptom, not a cause. She returns to Madrid with Ángel and resolves her various problems. In her absence, Ángel has been ghostwriting her contracted novels under the name Amanda Gris. The film ends as Leo and Ángel drink a toast in his apartment in a gesture that reminds her of the final scene of George Cukor's *Rich and Famous.*

Almodóvar's layering of a range of themes within a single plot is much in evidence in *The Flower of My Secret.* The three principal thematic threads woven together are melodrama, now treated as a theme rather than a narrative style; urban space, refocused as a city/country tension; and, perhaps most centrally, the struggle for authorial creativity in a world ordered by the aesthetics of mass culture. Almodóvar's heroine is trapped in a series of demands from her editor that are at odds with her evolving emotions and outlook. Although hired to write *novelas rosa* (literally, pink novels), she says that the turmoil of her personal life makes those novels "come out black." Her editor reminds her of the contractual obligations that do not allow her creative license. Her novels are only to contain "brilliant sunlight, urban housing developments, government bureaucrats or ministers as protagonists, yuppies.

Almodóvar directing Marisa Paredes
in a scene from *The Flower of My Secret*.
Courtesy of the Filmoteca Española.

Nothing political, no social consciousness, all the illegitimate children you want, and, of course, a happy ending" (Almodóvar, *La flor* 75).

As in Leo's business contract, melodrama is treated not as an authentic emotional state but as a series of marketable narrative conventions. Leo's responses to her failed marriage are viewed by Paco and Betty as mere theatrics, a false sensibility pulled from her novels that has immobilized her own life. Unlike the earlier use of melodrama in *Dark Habits* and *What Have I Done to Deserve This?* Almodóvar distances his audience and his character from the negative force of a melodramatic imagination. He fashions his heroine initially in much the same way that he develops the character of Pepa in *Women on the Verge*. Leo is introduced visually through extreme close-ups in an early scene when she is asleep in bed. These shots give her facial features—make-up, eyes and eyebrows, hair—a theatrical quality that recalls close-ups of the face of Joan Crawford, another melodramatic movie intertext used to characterize Pepa.

As in *Women on the Verge*, melodramatic excess is represented as a scenario out of which characters may exit as though exiting a theatrical scene. We see this from the start of the film, where a pattern of disrupted melodrama is established. The prologue involves two representatives of the Organ Donors Center enacting a playlet in which they attempt to persuade a distraught mother (Kiti Manver) to donate the organs of her comatose son. There is a pause in the scene as the grieving mother sobs. The dramatic intensity of the moment is broken as the camera slowly pans to the left to reveal the scene as a videotaped enactment that is part of a seminar Betty is running to train workers promoting organ transplants. The camera cuts to Leo's bedroom as she sleeps; the visual jump creates a thematic bridge between staged melodrama and Leo as a melodramatic character. We then return to the end of the rehearsal in Betty's seminar, amidst a postenactment discussion among the actors as Manver asks Betty if she is not perhaps exaggerating, in effect, "overacting." The question introduces the concept of emotional excess in melodrama as artifice to be modulated for effect.

The self-conscious staging of the organ-donor scene prepares us for the process of Leo's self-distancing from the paralyzing emotional responses that have ensnared her in a melodrama of her own design. Inspired by the use of the telephone as a stage prop in *Women on the Verge*, Almodóvar uses the phone insistently to disrupt Leo's descent into melodramatic emotions. When, having drifted into sleep after swallowing half a bottle of tranquilizers, she is aroused by the phone voice of her mother, the telephone literally saves her from her theatricalized suicide. Later, her angry confrontation with Betty is interrupted by another phone call, again from her mother, who has just had a terrible argument with her daughter and son-in-law.

The textual project of dislodging Leo from her melodramatic imagination is intimately linked to the rebirth of her creative energy as a writer. Ángel assigns her the task of writing a review attacking Amanda Gris's latest novel, which Leo does, tellingly, by criticizing the use of trite melodramatic conventions. The criticism represents Leo's self-rebuke of her own sensibility that she has channeled into her fictional writing. Her literary criticism, negotiated through the agency of Ángel as her editor and alter ego, mirrors the larger process of Leo distancing herself from melodrama.

Mazierska and Rascaroli describe the Madrid of *Flower* as "a truly melodramatic city" (45). Though "not filmed in hyper-emphatic tones . . . the emergence of melodrama in the film strongly influences the way in which the city is viewed" (46). They situate Leo's mood swings in the urban setting that surrounds her: her larger-than-life pain embodied in the morning wind that blows her window open in her first appearance; children playing in the courtyard below her apartment, whose presence underscores her solitude; the view of the glittering Gran Vía from the window of Ángel's apartment as he tells Leo that he likes her writing and wants to offer her a job reviewing books for *El País*. Although the treatment of the city is partially a reflection of the heroine's emotional state (as in many filmed melodramas, especially Douglas Sirk's films), we should note a significant difference here: the melodramatic motifs that earlier films emphasized to convey the emotional turmoil of the heroine now seem curiously formulaic and overstated in ways that suggest Almodóvar's design of distancing Leo not from the city but from a self-destructive melodramatic imagination. Her recuperation in the village, what Alejandro Yarza calls "the salve that cures the trauma imposed by the harshness of urban life" (170), suggests a soothing naturalness, emblemized by a landscape of yellow flowers and rolling fields of red earth that contrasts sharply with the artificial cityscape she has just left. At one key moment in the country, her mother remarks that Leo is "like a cow without a bell." The Spanish phrase, *una vaca sin cencerro,* Almodóvar tells us, is a local Andalusian expression that means an individual who has lost his or her direction in life. An early version of the script of *Flower of My Secret* was entitled "A Cow without a Bell."

Having recovered direction in her life, Leo can return to the city with a newfound self-confidence. Almodóvar includes a key scene with Ángel and Leo in the historic Plaza Mayor at night in which some of his earlier stylish evocation of Madrid is replayed. Ángel recalls Humphrey Bogart's line from *Casablanca,* "We will always have Paris," to suggest the recuperation of a positive affective bond with the city.

The film is constructed around Almodóvar's growing sense of the geo-cultural dynamic of contemporary Spain and its impact on individuals. He acknowledges as much when he describes the conception of *Flower* in a revealing note entitled "The Map," which appears in the expanded edition of the *Patty Diphusa* texts. He states that he built the film around what he called "la escena madre" (literally, and ironically, the "mother" scene) (178). The pivotal sequence of Leo's suicidal sleep contains a minor detail of décor, a map of Spain that hangs over her bed. Almodóvar describes it as a traditional "political" map of Spain that delineates the provinces and regions "with sky-blue waters, the kind they always put you in front of for school pictures" (177). The importance of the map derives from the ideological implications of its placement: "The image that you place above the headboard dominates the bedroom, protects our dreams, it guards the doors to our intimacy, it symbolizes what we believe in, something that instills confidence in us, shelters us, it protects us" (177). Though only visible for a fleeting instant, the image of the map prefigures Leo's physical and metaphoric journey across diverse cinematic and geocultural spaces, as these function to reposition her beyond the frame of melodrama and, in profound ways, to liberate her from the confining patriarchal ideology that is embodied in the map.

From a high-angle shot we see Leo stretched out across the bed, having just taken an overdose in response to Paco's announcement that there is no hope for reconciliation. He prefers to work with the Bosnian peace mission rather than respond to what Leo has called his domestic war. Paco's world is obviously one in which Spain is a sort of *patria chica* in the larger macro-region of Europe that seems to have clashed with the traditionalist Spain and thus symbolically has been one of the causes of the "civil war" that is his marriage.

Leo's suicide attempt is interrupted by her mother calling to tell her that, having fought with Leo's sister, she is returning to their provincial village. The amplified voice on the answering machine revives Leo, bringing her back to life. But just as Paco's appearance in a previous sequence challenged one version of unity—marriage—with a vision of Spain in Europe, the phone call suggests that the old tension of rural versus urban Spain, tradition versus modernity, again threatens the unity of the family.

Revived from her lethargic state, Leo goes to the corner bar for a cup of coffee. On the television monitor she looks at the image of the Mexican *bolero* singer Chavela Vargas singing "En el último trago" (The Last Drink), a song whose lyrics echo Leo's sense of abandonment but are notably devoid of her self-pity. Like the antimelodramatic pattern we have noted thus far, Vargas transforms the clichés of lovers separating from self-pity to simple resignation.

Tómate esta botella conmigo,
En el último trago nos vamos.
Quiero ver a qué sabe tu olvido.
Esta noche no voy a rogarte.
Esta noche te vas de veras.
Qué difícil tratar de olvidarte, aunque sepa que ya no me quieras.
Nada me han enseñado los años.
Siempre caigo en los mismos errores.
Otra vez a brindar con extraños y llorar por los mismos dolores.

[Have this last drink with me,
Let's have one for the road.
I want to know what your rejection tastes like.
Tonight I'm not going to beg you.
Tonight you're leaving for good.
How hard it is to try to forget you, even though I know that you don't
    love me anymore.
The years have taught me nothing.
I keep making the same mistakes.
Let's toast again with strangers and cry about the same heartaches.]

Leo begins to cry but recomposes herself and walks out of the bar into the street. She is thrust into a political demonstration of medical students protesting policies of the Felipe González government. She thus comes violently face to face with yet another notion of the Spanish nation in which democracy is not the mini-narrative of the melodramatic heroine but a broad sea of humanity. This is the first time an explicit Spanish political critique is presented in an Almodóvar film. The eruption of this brief political reference in *The Flower of My Secret* joins other references to negative aspects of Spanish contemporary social reality—unemployment, drug addiction, the social stereotypes against gypsies—that mark the beginning of a more emphatic depiction of Spanish social reality in Almodóvar's later work (Colmeiro 119). Amidst the agitated crowd, Leo, who is about to faint, is "saved" by a "guardian angel"—she literally falls into Ángel's waiting arms. As the strains of the

Cuban singer Bola de Nieve's "Ay amor" are heard, there is a gradual tracking across the Madrid sky to a window of a bedroom where Leo lies, now in Ángel's bed.

This sequence is not bracketed off with intertitles, as Almodóvar had originally planned. But the repetition of the bed—Leo's journey from her solitary bed to Ángel's—combined with the prefatory image of the map and the subsequent array of divergent motifs related to figurations of the community, gives the sequence the coherence of a geocultural allegory rooted in an eclectic array of cultural referents. The country-city dichotomy of action and the Spain-Europe opposition, present throughout the plot, are condensed into Leo's tension with onscreen characters: her mother and absented husband. These, in turn, are encoded as cinematic quotations: *Surcos* is alluded to in Leo's mother's announcement of her return to the village; and the mise-en-scène of the reunion of Ángel and Leo in the midst of the crowd recalls Ingrid Bergman and George Sanders embracing in the midst of a religious festival in the final scene of Roberto Rossellini's *Viaggio en Italia* (Voyage in Italy; 1948).

Against these Eurocentric tensions are juxtaposed the songs of the two Latin American artists, which underscore the melodramatic dimension of the heroine's identity while radically refiguring the otherwise fragmented map that is Leo's life. Challenging geography and even time—these are both extremely dated popular melodies that are well known by Spanish audiences—the singers are symbolic figures who speak from marginal social positions: those of gender, race, gayness, and colonialism. They suggest that the genres that confine Leo—literary, in the case of the *novelas rosa;* emotional, in her marriage; now even geopolitical, in the traditional map that hangs over her bed—are forms that constrict her spirit. Their presence, even as disembodied voices, suggests an acoustic imagination that here, and in the films to follow, refigures the map of Spain to include a broader Hispanic transnational community that had been excluded by the old patriarchal borders.

Marsha Kinder reads the itinerary suggested by the map sequence as the individual's and Spanish society's change of its own "imaginary": "Leo's love object changes from a lean, silent man of action like Paco to the fleshy, verbal, nurturing Ángel, who is more an alter ego than a lover. . . . *La flor* implies that it is also time for Spain to change its imaginary. It must reject the quixotic European obsessions of men like Paco and Felipe (González) and find renewal by looking at the specificity of 'el país' (the country itself) through new eyes" ("Refiguring" 16–17).

At the same time, within the context of the increasingly negative reception of *Kika,* the explicit treatment of Leo's crisis of creativity and its resolution in a return to her roots suggests a similar self-referential allegory for Almodóvar, a film author who, like Leo, recognizes himself as "a cow without a bell" (Colmeiro 126). Again playing with opaque self-reference, Almodóvar says of *The Flower of My Secret,* "This is my most Manchegan film, an unconscious return to my roots, and the primary root is the mother" (*La flor* 165).

The Flower of My Secret is thus a pivotal work in Almodóvar's development. In the immediate context of his commercial filmmaking, it suggests a recovery of the "touch" that many reviewers claimed he had lost in his recent work. Read retrospectively as a statement of his credo for films to come, it can be seen as Almodóvar's disengagement from Madrid as the exclusive locus of his creativity, a return to his roots, the rumination of an author whose need to "evolve" had jeopardized his connection with a popular audience.

Live Flesh (1997)

One of the themes underlying the dramatic and narrative development of *The Flower of My Secret* is that of individuals' confinement in social structures that restrict their spirit. Leo is trapped in a melodramatic plot that disables her personal and creative life. Significantly, there is a comic hint early in the film of the physical equivalent of this spiritual confinement. She has been wearing boots that Paco gave her, to which she has a sentimental attachment; now she finds that she cannot get them off. She even enlists the help of a young man on the street, who turns out to be the son of her literary agent, Alicia. Finally, her best friend Betty helps her remove the boots, but not before lecturing her on the disorder of her emotional life, thereby allowing us to see the tight-fitting boots as a metaphor for the psychological and artistic confinements in which Leo finds herself.

In his next film, *Carne trémula* (Live Flesh), Almodóvar literalizes physical confinement in a plot about David (Javier Bardem), a paraplegic who is trapped in his body. His rival, Víctor (Liberto Rabal), has spent three years in prison for allegedly firing the gun that paralyzed David and now appears to be stalking David's wife, Elena (Francesca Neri). This story of sexual attraction and paralyzed bodies is framed by the historical narrative that begins with the circumstance of Víctor's birth on a public bus in downtown Madrid on the very night in 1970 when the Franco government declared a national state of emergency, suspending all constitutional rights. It ends twenty-six years later with the pregnant Elena, now Víctor's wife, going into labor not far from where Víctor was born. In this way, personal narratives of physical confinement are framed by the more expansive historical narrative of Spain's deliverance from the Franco regime's political confinement.

Warmly received by Spanish and international audiences, *Live Flesh* was generally viewed as further confirmation of Almodóvar's creative reemergence after the difficulties of the early nineties. Some Spanish critics, like Carlos Boyero in Madrid's *El Mundo* and Ángel Fernández-Santos of *El País,* who had earlier criticized Almodóvar's presumed incompetent crafting of plots, effusively praised *Live Flesh* for its tight and rigorous script. That script was not Almodóvar's sole invention but a collaboration with two other film writers, Ray Loriga and Jorge Guerri-caechevarría. This was the first time since *Matador,* another male-centered narrative, that Almodóvar shared script-writing credits. The film is also his first adaptation of a literary source, Ruth Rendell's psychological thriller *Live Flesh.* Almodóvar acknowledges that all that remains of the Rendell novel is the basic plot situation of the two male protagonists, David, a police detective, and Víctor, the man falsely accused of wounding and paralyzing him.

Steven Marsh notes that this is also Almododóvar's "first film to explore heterosexual masculinity with any degree of seriousness" (54). In Almodóvar's transformation of the Rendell story into a film about flesh and the body, Chris Perriam discerns the underlying "queer way" the film characterizes David and Víctor as "antagonists with the woman left out" (107). According to Perriam, in that transformation, "Bardem's character and Rabal's are embroiled in a contest, the premise of which is that bodies matter, that they are deployed in the strenuous performance of being a man" (105).

Almodóvar relocates the Rendell plot to Madrid, adding a framing story in which, for the first time in his films, political contexts figure prominently. The frame is set during the Christmas season in Madrid at two different moments, one in January 1970, and the other twenty-six years later. The prologue details the circumstances in which Isabel (Penélope Cruz), a prostitute, gives birth to Víctor on a bus on the very night that the spokesman of the Franco government, Manuel Fraga Iribarne, announces the suspension of constitutional rights as a response to terrorist activities.

Twenty years later, Víctor is a lowly pizza deliveryman trying to arrange a date with Elena, a drug addict with whom he once slept but who now rejects his advances. There is a scuffle in her apartment, a gun is fired, and two police detectives, Sancho (Pepe Sancho) and his young partner, David (Javier Bardem), arrive. Víctor resists arrest, and in the ensuing struggle, after Elena escapes, another gun is fired, and David falls to the floor wounded. Víctor is arrested and jailed for assaulting a detective. Later, during his confinement, Víctor sees the wheelchair-bound David playing in a televised basketball game during the 1992 Barcelona Paralympics. He spots Elena in the audience and rekindles his obsession, but it is now a desire for revenge against her. Upon release from prison, he goes looking for Elena, who is now married to David. Locating her in a day-care center for homeless children, Víctor quickly signs on as a volunteer.

Upset by what he thinks is Víctor's stalking of his wife, David threatens him. Meanwhile, Víctor has met Clara (Angela Molina), Sancho's wife, and has an affair with her. His interest, as he makes clear, is not emotional but purely sexual. He is still sexually inexperienced, boasting that, even after prison, he is still HIV-negative. Now he simply wants to learn the techniques of making love so he can impress Elena. Eventually, he learns from Clara that it was her violent and abusive husband, Sancho, who intentionally fired the gun as revenge against David, whom he sensed was having an affair with her. In a later confrontation with David, Víctor stuns him by repeating this information. When Víctor tells Elena, she feels responsible for his imprisonment, and the two share passionate love. Elena immediately confesses her infidelity to David. Angered and humiliated, David seeks vengeance against Víctor by telling the drunken Sancho of Víctor's affair with Clara. When Clara attempts to leave the abusive Sancho, he stalks her to Víctor's cottage. The spouses confront each other with guns, and both die.

There follows a time jump to another Christmas. Elena and Víctor are now married. David writes Elena from Miami, where he continues his basketball career. The film ends on another holiday night that recalls Víctor's birth. Víctor rushes his pregnant wife to the hospital. En route, he speaks to his unborn child: "You're lucky, you are, little kid! You don't know how things have changed. Spain lost its fear a long time ago."

Live Flesh is distinctive among Almodóvar's films in that it is completely devoid of the comic gags that so regularly punctuate his earlier cinematic stories. As the title suggests, the story is about sexual bodies. The original Rendell title actually referred to flesh-eating bacteria. Here, however, it takes on an erotic connotation. The theme of the sexual body and its confinement is developed first in the ironic intertext of Luis Buñuel's *Ensayo de un crimen* (The Criminal Life of Archibaldo de la Cruz; 1955), which Víctor watches on television in Elena's apartment on the fateful night in 1990 when David is shot. Elena has passed out on the sofa, and Víctor is watching the movie when he is interrupted by David and Sancho. We see two clips from the Buñuel film: the early sequence in which a stray bullet accidentally kills the young Archibaldo's governess, and a later scene in which Archi burns a mannequin of Lavinia, the woman who spurned him. The clips appear as an interior duplication of the story of Víctor and Elena and the obstacles that intervene to thwart their sexual union: An initial stray bullet leads to Víctor's incarceration and his separation from his love; Archie's illusion of his destructive power over Lavinia prefigures Víctor's later illusion of his own sexual power to force Elena into submission.

Claudia Schaefer, however, offers an ingenious decipherment of the film-within-the-film that fits with the geocultural dynamic of *Live Flesh* and its historical-political frame. She posits her reading on the interpolation of the figure of Buñuel into contemporary Spanish cultural discourse as a symbolic recovery of an exiled political past (110). Steven Marsh notes, in a similar context, that the cast of *Live Flesh* included actors like Angela Molina, Pilar Bardem, and Liberto Rabal, the grandson of Francisco Rabal, all of whom were associated with Buñuel (66). The choice of *Ensayo de un crimen* is significant in that, according to Buñuel, it is the story of the individual's misrecognition of the past. In the first scene, the governess's shooting is linked to the historical image of the Mexican Revolution and the misperceived origins of male power.

Analogously, as Schaeffer argues, the story of the adult Víctor is con-nected to the political narrative of the final years of the Franco dictator-ship (126–27). Buñuel's film-within-Almodóvar's-film emphasizes that *Live Flesh* is essentially a narrative about looking back and fits into the broader patterns of Spanish national cultural recovery through cinema and narrative of the 1990s (110).

In confirmation of Schaeffer's general reading of the film, Almodó-var notes that although he elected not to evoke the images of Francoist Spain throughout much of his career, he now chose to do so, and in this particular way, because of the apparently circular process through which Spain's political past seemed to have returned. He refers to his inclusion of the voice of Fraga Iribarne, whom Almodóvar describes as "a man who today remains the president of the Galician Regional government and who soon will present himself for reelection. He is founder of the Partido Popular, which is the actual government in power. It astounded me that the man who announced such a monstrous thing is not only still alive, but he remains involved in Spanish political life. In his voice, his horrible voice, he speaks poorly, what you hear in the film, and for Span-iards, perhaps it may come as a surprise to recognize him. . . . Twenty years ago my revenge against Franco lay in not recognizing his existence, his memory, in making films as if he had never walked the earth. Now I think it's not good to forget that time, it's worth remembering that in the final analysis, it wasn't that long ago" (Strauss, *Conversaciones* 154).

In the larger context of Almodóvar's career, what stands out in *Live Flesh* are the temporal and spatial structures inscribed in the film that seek to situate the contemporary political culture of 1990s Spain with Spanish historical processes. In this regard, the film marks Almodóvar's first important revision of his own political posture of *pasotismo* and sets the groundwork for his subsequent development of the historical narrative of *Bad Education. Live Flesh* is intentionally constructed to be self-consciously historical, the first truly historical narrative of his filmography. The plot is built on a series of seemingly disconnected historical moments—1970, 1990, 1992, and 1996—but is designed to bring the audience, as Almodóvar says, to reflect on the concept of na-tional political history. As the framing story suggests, a historical causality shapes this curiously genealogical narrative. Shot on the eve of the 1996 Spanish general elections, which would bring Fraga Iribarne's Partido

Popular to power, the film's depiction of Víctor's genealogy intentionally suggests a spatial and temporal circularity in which the voice of Fraga underscores the proximity of Spain's political past to its present.

That historical circularity similarly governs the film's urban mise-en-scène, which continually suggests notions of center and periphery. The 1970 action begins at the pensión of Doña Centro (Pilar Bardem) in the center of the city. Víctor, who has been marginalized by his birth and imprisonment, returns to Madrid to occupy his mother's house in the Ventilla district, a peripheral barrio inhabited largely by immigrants from southern Spain. Víctor's cottage is often shot against the rising KIO Towers in the distance, a striking urban landmark that locates these marginalized characters in relation to the icons of a modern Spain still under construction. As Marsh notes, the towers, originally named for Kuwaiti Investment Office, were renamed La Puerta de Europa (Doorway to Europe), underscoring modern Spain's dream of cultural and economic rapprochement with Europe. Given the squalor of the area, the imposing image of the towers as a backdrop to some of the film's action serves to mock that aspiration by exposing the harsh economic reality of the barrio and of Spain's underclass (57). Finally, in the return to the recognizable Puerta de Sol district of Madrid for the final Christmas sequence, Almodóvar suggests historical circularity of action, from urban center to periphery, back to the downtown center in the final images. Almodóvar situates his striking political framework through that expression of the circular motif of the film (Edwards 167–68), linking it to the theme of confinement and, with the overt symbolic suggestion of Víctor and his child as "Christmas children," to the theme of hope for the future.

Live Flesh, which became the second biggest box-office hit in Spain in 1997, just behind Alex de la Iglesia's comic *Airbag*, was marketed abroad as a "sensuous thriller." Richard Corliss's review in *Time* was highlighted in the MGM/United Artists publicity campaign, which successfully marketed the film to the all-important U.S. audience. Corliss noted: "Almodóvar is that rare moviemaker who still thinks that sex and love are as important as a space invasion or a sinking ship." Though structured around a rigorous formulation of Spanish cultural, political, and historical specificity, *Live Flesh* engaged an international as well as a national audience through its use of genre formulas: a tense sex drama involving narratives of adultery, male competition, and dramatic shoot-outs. Almodóvar's cultivation of this kind of historicized narrative reflects his evolving conception of his cinema. The film was chosen for the final screening at the 1997 Lincoln Center Film Festival in New York and went on to receive strong critical praise in the U.S. media.

All about My Mother (1999)

There are obvious formal connections between Almodóvar's next film, *Todo sobre mi madre* (All about My Mother), and *Live Flesh*. Both reveal a sense of characters rooted in urban space. In *Live Flesh* that spatial anchoring is Madrid, although one brief scene takes place in Barcelona. By contrast, *All about My Mother* moves from Madrid to the Catalan capital as its principal setting. In both films, locale becomes a way of characterizing story: in *Live Flesh*, the drama of the national community is set in Madrid, while the narrative of alternate constructions of communities that is at the heart of *All about My Mother* is located in Spain's Second City, Barcelona. In both films there is the familiar theme of the formation of a new family. Finally, in order to tell his story, for both films Almodóvar devises a series of time jumps introduced through intertitles superimposed over images. In particular, Manuela (Cecilia Roth), the protagonist of *All about My Mother*, is seen going back and forth by train between Madrid and Barcelona as intertitles announce time shifts.

For all of their surface similarities, however, a genealogical break in the conception of *All about My Mother* sets it apart from *Live Flesh*. In an interview with Frédéric Strauss, Almodóvar says: "*The Flower of My Secret* is the generating film source for *All about My Mother*. Manuela's story already appears in *Flower*. What I've done as a film director with *All about My Mother* is the continuation of *The Flower of My Secret*, making a little bridge over *Live Flesh*. . . . It's as if the film were the engine that generated *All about My Mother*" (*Conversaciones* 180). He is obviously referring to the curious fact that both *The Flower of My Secret* and *All about My Mother* begin with almost identical scenes of the videotaping of a rehearsal in which a medical team tries to persuade a distraught woman to donate the organs of her recently deceased son.

Details of *Flower* prefigure the plot of Manuela's situation in *All about My Mother* (Kinder, "Reinventing" 250–51).

The image of the mother as a creative source also unites the films. In *The Flower of My Secret,* Leo's mother is the catalyst for her daughter's spiritual regeneration. In *All about My Mother,* Manuela embodies the maternal. She becomes the source of inspiration to her son, giving him Truman Capote's book of essays, *Music for Chameleons,* and a theater ticket to see Tennessee Williams's *A Streetcar Named Desire.* In Barcelona, after her son's death, she chides the nun, Sister Rosa, for not accepting her mother. Finally, she cares for Sister Rosa's son as though he were her own.

Another key aspect of the unity between the two works lies in their geocultural realignments. Beginning with *Flower,* Almodóvar's narrative space moves beyond Madrid, a revision of the lines of the old geography that had shaped his cinema up to the mid-nineties. In *All about My Mother,* for the first time in Almodóvar's films, there is a nearly complete break with Madrid. After the initial sequence and the death of Manuela's son, all the action shifts to Barcelona. A new linkage through dialogue alludes to geographical sites outside of Spain: Paris and Argentina. Years earlier, Manuela and her husband Estéban, later transformed into Lola, emigrated to Paris from their native Argentina. The unspoken assumption is that, like many Argentines of the late 1970s, they fled their homeland in the wake of the "Proceso" (or "Dirty War"), the series of murders, tortures, and "disappearances" of individuals, principally younger people perceived as dissidents. On the day that Rosa delivers her baby, the third Estéban, Manuela remarks that this is a happy day, not only because of the birth but also because General Videla, one of the leaders of the brutal military dictatorship in Argentina, has been arrested. These political intertexts and the new range of non-Madrid geographic references contribute to the sense of a newly emerging style and spirit in *All about My Mother.* Like *Live Flesh,* it is more rooted in a sense of historical change than earlier Almodóvar films.

Manuela, a single mother and nurse, works as a coordinator at an organ-transplant center in Madrid. She lives with her son, Estéban (Eloy Azorín), an aspiring writer. For his seventeenth birthday, Manuela gives Estéban the volume of essays by Truman Capote and tickets for the theatrical performance of his favorite actress, Huma Rojo (Marisa Paredes), in *A Streetcar Named Desire*. After the performance, as mother and son wait outside the theater to get the actress's autograph, Manuela reveals to Estéban that she once performed in that same play with his father. Estéban wishes he knew more about his father, and Manuela promises that, as another birthday gift, when they return home she will tell him all about his father. Suddenly, Huma comes out and, with her partner, Nina Cruz (Candela Peña), quickly rushes into a taxi. Estéban runs after them in the rain and is struck down by a passing vehicle. Grief-stricken, Manuela consents to donate her deceased son's organs.

Determined to fulfill her son's final wish, Manuela goes to Barcelona in search of the man she had loved and then abandoned eighteen years earlier, the father of her son. Estéban (Toni Cantó) has become a transsexual and is now known as Lola, La Piconera. In Barcelona, Manuela reencounters Agrado (Antonia San Juan), a transsexual prostitute and friend of Lola, who puts her in contact with a nun who does charitable work with the prostitutes of the area. Sister Rosa (Penélope Cruz) claims not to have seen Lola in four months. As events evolve, however, Rosa confesses that she is pregnant with Lola's baby and infected with his AIDS virus.

Manuela nurses Rosa through her pregnancy, and a baby boy, the new Estéban, is born infected. Rosa dies in childbirth, and Lola appears at her funeral, a pathetic and physically weakened figure. At an arranged meeting with Lola, Manuela tells him of his first son's birth, life, and death. The news shatters the already despondent Lola. Manuela has arranged for Rosa's own mother to take the baby. The third Estéban is miraculously cured of the disease.

The title of *All about My Mother* derives from an early scene in which, on the eve of his birthday, Estéban is watching a movie on television with his mother, Mankiewicz's *All about Eve*. The film appears in the Spanish-dubbed version, *Eva al desnudo* (Eve Unveiled, or Eve Naked). Estéban comments that the title is incorrect and offers as a translation, *Todo sobre Eva*. Later, as they wait in the rain for Huma Rojo, Estéban says he would like to know "todo sobre mi padre" (all about my father). The substitution of the father for the mother, Eve, suggests the pairing of the themes of maternity and paternity throughout the film. Even before the performance, we see Estéban sitting in a bar across from the theater writing notes, seemingly about his mother. He looks across the street and sees her waiting anxiously in front of a huge billboard advertising the play, an image that consists solely of Huma Rojo's head. The juxtaposition of Estéban's creative inclinations, the view of his mother, and the imposing image of Huma Rojo combine to underscore the concept of the pairing of the figure of maternity with creativity, another theme that threads through the plot. Later, when Manuela is drawn to seek out Huma backstage after another performance of *Streetcar*, she appears wearing a raincoat that is strikingly similar to that worn by Eve Harrington (Ann Baxter) in the Mankiewicz film. Huma hires Manuela as her assistant, and, as did Eve, Manuela subsequently goes onstage as an understudy for Huma's lover, Nina. The only scenes from *Streetcar* that are dramatized in the play-within-the-film show a pregnant Stella Kowalski, her brutish husband, Stanley, and Blanche Dubois. This triangle of the family in crisis was the play in which Manuela and the absented Estéban performed years earlier in Argentina. The film pivots around this mirroring process of life imitating art. As Manuela works as Nina's understudy in the play, she is able to sustain the theatrical illusion of a family. Outside the theater, the idea of family undergoes a similar process of regeneration with an unexpected pairing—Sister Rosa and Lola—replacing the conventional mother and father.

An essential part of that regeneration lies in the concept of maternity, posed in *All about My Mother* in the classical cultural terms of giving birth and nurturing. These are roles immediately identified with Manuela as mother and nurse from the credit sequence. Her identity as a nurse is also closely identified with performance, as we see her interpret the role of the mother in the organ-transplant rehearsal. The scene parallels the subsequent plot and also links maternity with the notion of regeneration. We see maternity also connected to the idea of the recycling of organs, giving new life through organ transplant. Maternity is associated with the idea of the feminine as performance—Manuela first enacts the role of the distraught mother and then becomes the distraught mother. In Barcelona, when she replaces Nina in the Williams play, she performs the role of the pregnant Stella Kowalski.

The role of the family in the film is structured around the pairing of the improbable couple, Manuela and Lola. Late in the film, Manuela brings the baby Estéban to meet his father, now in drag, in a bar near the home of Rosa's parents. As Almodóvar notes: "This atypical family evokes for me the variety of families that are possible in these times. If there is something that characterizes the end of the twentieth century it's the rupture of the traditional family. Now you can form families with other members, other ties, other biological relations that need to be respected. The most important thing is that the members of the family love each other" (Strauss, *Conversaciones* 162). The sentiment harks back to *Law of Desire,* in which the traditional family is refigured through the gay brother Pablo, his transsexual lesbian sister Tina, and the child Ada, whose mother is a transsexual (Bibi Andersen).

Through Manuela's "mothering," Rosa, a figure of charitable nurturing, is able to give birth to the third Estéban, suggesting a reworking of the trinity (Rosa, Manuela, Estéban) within which two women jointly share the mothering role in order to creatively make possible a new Estéban. What is especially noteworthy in the complex range of thematic possibilities of creativity engendered by this reworking of the traditional family is its crossing of geographic as well as gender barriers. The third Estéban, the child of Lola and Rosa, is of Spanish and Argentine lineage, collapsing geography within genealogy and biology. As Marsha Kinder has noted, the dramatized request for the organ donation, which serves as a prologue to both *All about My Mother* and *The Flower of My Secret,* the first two parts of the "brain-dead trilogy," help mark the common themes of "loss, growth, and recovery" ("Reinventing" 254).

In the intricate weave of surrogate and refigured identities within the family, patriarchy is resemanticized, principally through Lola, the man who would be a woman—the woman who is the father of both Estébans. Similarly, maternity and surrogate motherhood are joined to the idea of performances of maternity and the film's emphasis on the identification of women as actresses. From the early scene in which Manuela gives her son Capote's *Music for Chameleons,* role playing, changing identities, and the seemingly oxymoronic notion of a simulation of authenticity begin to develop as a cluster of related concepts. The chameleon, a figure capable of change, is the central structural-artistic motif of the film. We see this early on in the members of the organ-donation center performing as victims and hospital representatives. In a bitterly ironic twist, Manuela goes from performing the role of the grieving woman to being the grieving mother. This inversion of reality and performance is repeated in the image Estéban sees of his mother waiting in front of the theater against the bigger-than-life image of Huma Rojo. Manuela, who has played Stella in the past, will repeat the performance and then follow it offstage as surrogate mother to Rosa.

Finally, the figures of the chameleon and the simulations of authenticity come together in Barcelona. In an early scene in which she brings Manuela to meet Rosa, Agrado wears a stylish red suit. Manuela asks if it is a real Chanel design, to which Agrado laughs. "With all the hunger in the world, who could afford an authentic Chanel?" Thus, for the first time the theme of authenticity is explicitly introduced in dialogue. Later, the in-transit transsexual Agrado delivers a speech to the theater audience after the performance of *Streetcar* has been canceled. She says: "They call me Agrado because all I want to do is make life agreeable for others. Besides agreeable, I'm also very authentic." She then proceeds to detail each of the surgical procedures she has undergone so far in her transformation into a female, each, like her two seventy-thousand-peseta breasts, a sign of her "authenticity." Her final line is key to her identity, of course, but also to the concept of authenticity: "A woman is more authentic the more she resembles what she dreams herself to be" (*una mujer es más auténtica cuanto más se parece a lo que ha soñado de sí misma*). The female body, the body of the mother, the whore, the transsexual, and, finally, the quintessential expression of creativity, the actress, ultimately unify the film.

Creativity, understood as the authoring of one's self, an idea that germinates from *Tie Me Up! Tie Me Down!* and *High Heels,* is here given centrality, as it relates to the second Estéban's self-willed eclectic literary authorship. He is a Spaniard of Argentine descent whose two literary inspirations are gay American writers: Truman Capote and Tennessee Williams. A different geocultural sense of creativity proposed in the new genealogical line is implied in Lola's political backstory. He is an Argentine exile who fathered a new generation through his sexual contact with a Spanish nun to produce a new transnational Hispanic family. By linking the conception of *All about My Mother* to *The Flower of My Secret,* Almodóvar suggests a creative genealogy informing his work that defies the obvious logic of genre, gender, and geography.

All about My Mother is dedicated to actresses, not only in its general formulation of plot but also in the formal dedication with which the film ends: "Dedicated to the actresses who play actresses—specifically

Bette Davis, Gena Rowlands, and Romy Schneider." Almodóvar claims that he could have expanded the list to include Gloria Swanson, Judy Garland, Lana Turner, and Ava Gardner, among others (Almodóvar, *Todo*). In this sense, the film's open ending and dedication tie it back into the stagey world of movie melodramas he had integrated into his previous films. Even more importantly, however, Agrado's performance monologue embodies the themes of desire and identity. In contrast to the devastatingly nihilistic finale of *Kika,* where the vision of Youcalli is made the site of double murders, the ending of *All about My Mother* reveals the creative generation of new identities, new personal and social relations, as well as the sense of rebirth.

All about My Mother has received more awards and honors than any film in motion-picture history, Spanish or otherwise. These include an Oscar for the Best Foreign Language Film, Best Director, and Ecumenical Award at Cannes; the French César for Best Foreign Film; a Golden Globe for Best Foreign Film; a British Academy Award; a British Independent Film Award for Best Foreign Film, and a Twelfth Annual European Film Award. Though this international recognition was important, it must have come also as a vindication for Almodóvar to receive similarly effusive praise at home, where *All about My Mother* received seven Goyas from the Spanish Film Academy, including Best Film, Best Director, and Best Leading Actress for Cecilia Roth.

Days after the triumph of the Oscar, Román Gubern, Spain's preeminent historian of Spanish cinema, wrote an appreciation of the event for *El Mundo* in which he reminded Spaniards that Almodóvar's universality derives precisely from his localism. That is, the rootedness in a historical moment of *La movida* and the underground culture that had come into existence as resistance and reaction to the forty years of dictatorship. What is most striking about the tribute is its suggestion of a vindication of all the cultural marginalizations Spanish artists had endured, not only from the outside world, but also from within Spain's borders.

Talk to Her and *Bad Education*

In the euphoric months that followed the shower of international awards, Almodóvar confided to an interviewer: "*All about My Mother* gave me a confidence in myself, but now I yearn do to things I've never done before, but it's an idea that turns out to be exciting and scary at the same time" (Strauss, *Conversaciones* 176). This new sense of self-assurance resulted in a pair of films composed almost simultaneously, both of which grew out of the experience of *All about My Mother.*

Hable con ella (Talk to Her; 2002) opens with the image of the salmon-colored stage curtain with which *All about My Mother* ends. As Almodóvar explains, "The characters of *All about My Mother* were actresses, imposters, or women with the skill to act both on stage and off; *Talk to Her* follows narrators, people who tell stories about themselves; men who talk to whoever can hear them and, above all, to those who can't hear them" (*Hable*). In this regard, *Talk to Her* appears to be the formal extension of *All about My Mother,* although it focuses on the stories told by men rather than women. In turn, *Talk to Her* and the film that follows it, *La mala educación* (Bad Education; 2004), although on the surface radically different, actually share a number of structural features that suggest the commonality of their script creation (Strauss, *Conversaciones* 176). Each is constructed from an earlier text around which a new plot is developed to "frame" the original source material. In the case of *Talk to Her,* the pre-text is the script of a silent movie, *Amante menguante* (The Shrinking Lover). *Bad Education* is constructed around a story that Almodóvar wrote in the 1970s, which he describes as "a furious tale in which I took revenge on the religious education that I had received in a school run by priests twenty years earlier" (Almodóvar, *La mala educación* 11).

The protagonists also share a common genealogy—Benigno (Javier Cámara) in *Talk to Her* and Juan (Gael García Bernal) in *Bad Education* are both inspired by Patricia Highsmith characters. Almodóvar describes Benigno as modeled after the psychopathic character from Highsmith's 1960 novel *This Sweet Sickness* (Strauss, *Entretien* 190). The protagonist is a man "so obsessed with his ex-lover that he creates another identity . . . through whom he feels able to satisfy his repressed desires and live out his dreams of domestic bliss with the fantasy image" (Wilson 210). In *Bad Education,* Juan is a more prototypical Highsmith character, modeled after Tom Ripley as portrayed by Alain Delon in René Clérment's version of *The Talented Mister Ripley, Plein Soleil* (1960). "Like the Delon character, Juan is an unscrupulous criminal whose beautiful face enables him to mask his true nature" (Strauss, *Entretien* 190). Beyond these common features, however, Almodóvar develops two strikingly different films.

Talk to Her (2002)

For all the apparent complexity of its multiple narratives, the basic plot of *Talk to Her* is remarkably simple, certainly in contrast to Almodóvar's previous work. Two total strangers, Marco and Benigno, find themselves sitting side by side at a theatrical performance of the Pina Bausch dance company's production of "Café Müller." Marco (Darío Grandinetti), a travel writer in his forties, is teary-eyed, moved by Bausch's choreography and the Henry Purcell music from "The Fairie Queen." Benigno (Javier Cámara), a nurse, is also moved by the ballet, and he notices Marco's emotional response. Months later, again by chance, their paths cross in the corridor of a sanitarium where Benigno works caring for a comatose patient, Alicia (Leonor Watling), a dance student. Marco's lover, Lydia (Rosario Flores), a bullfighter, has been gored in a *corrida* and is also in a coma. Over the ensuing months, the men become friends. Through a series of flashbacks, we learn how Marco met and fell in love with Lydia after he interviewed her for a newspaper story and how Benigno pursued Alicia, whom he first saw practicing in a dance studio across the street from the house where he lived caring for his invalid mother.

Marco is perplexed by Benigno's insistence that even though Alicia and Lydia are comatose, people should still talk to them as though they were awake and conscious. When Marco protests that they are brain-dead, the seemingly slow-witted Benigno insists that women in general are enigmatic and that men should talk to them. The gesture of talking to a person who cannot answer, actually an external monologue, returns us to the sequence in *Law of Desire* in which Tina is involved in the rehearsal of Cocteau's "La voix humaine." As in *Law of Desire*, the human voice, instead of signifying communication, becomes a mark of the characters' isolation. Mark Allinson notes that Benigno's confusion between mere talking and a true reciprocity between two people is one of the driving forces of the film (Allinson, *Un laberinto* 115).

When Lydia dies, Marco becomes interested in the comatose Alicia. At one point, nurses discover that Alicia is pregnant. Since she could not have consented to sexual contact in her comatose state, this is considered a rape for which Benigno is charged and imprisoned. Marco maintains his communication with Benigno. Alicia comes out of her coma, her return to consciousness apparently triggered by childbirth. Benigno commits suicide. Yet, despite this depressing circumstance, the film ends with hope as Marco and Alicia find themselves together at a performance of the Pina Bausch group performing the airy "Masurca Fogo," a dance of sexual union.

The final dialogue of the film is between Marco and Katerina (Geraldine Chaplin), Alicia's dance teacher and friend. When they meet in the theater during the intermission of "Masurca Fogo," Marco promises to explain to her about Benigno: "It is all much simpler than you imagine." She responds, "Nothing is simple. I teach dance, and nothing is simple." Beyond the plot, her words seem to allude to the film itself. That apparent simplicity comes from the way the two dances frame the narrative and mirror the general lines of the story: In "Café Müller" we see two female somnambulists moving wildly through an empty café; a man continually rearranges the furniture to prevent the women from falling. In "Masurca Fogo" a young couple is united in a verdant setting that suggests the Garden of Eden. The first dance prefigures the ways in which Benigno has been consumed by caring for Alicia's welfare; the second appears to reflect Marco's final union with Alicia and the audience's witnessing the creation of a new love (Strauss, *Entretien* 210).

Marsha Kinder suggests that, positioned as a prologue to the film, the "Café Müller" sequence enables us to read the movements of the characters in the subsequent story as dance. "The daily grooming and massaging of Alicia's inert body, the ritualistic dressing of Lydia in her suit of lights, the contrasting movements of matador and toro in the corrida, Marco's methodical killing of a snake, and the graceful gliding of an anonymous male body through a swimming pool—all these actions are transformed into dance" ("Reinventing" 255).

The simplicity of these dance scenes that symbolically express Benigno and Marco's relation to the two comatose women is undercut by a chain of ironic reversals of identity in the narrative: The bullfighter is a woman, and the nurse is a man. Though it is never openly stated by either character, the emotional bonding between the two men is continually read by hospital and prison officials as a gay relationship. Finally, Marco replaces Benigno in his apartment, in his very bed, and in his imagined relationship with Alicia. When she finally awakens and sees Marco, Alicia is drawn to him as if they had known each other earlier, which they had not. The process of the evolving narrative, a loosely mounted collage of dramatic scenes that fluidly merges moments from the past with those of the present, produces this shuffling of characters in which the conventional boundaries that define their identities and stories are blurred and weakened.

Gender, which is never questioned in the film except to deride the psychiatrist's view of Benigno's presumed homosexuality, is also presented as fluid. We see this in the gender reversals of Benigno and Lydia's professions. In both instances, the gender switch implies a cultural modernization within which traditional gendered professions are seen as mobile. This is especially true for Lydia, whose name in Spanish means "bullfighting." During a television interview, she is even asked about gender bias among *toreros*. The bullfight, the quintessential expression of atavistic and violent Spain, had earlier undergone revision in Almodóvar's *Matador*. Here, as Allinson notes, the female bullfighter suggests the progressive change in bullfighting as women gain access to a profession previously dominated by men (*Un laberinto* 118).

The fluidity of gender mirrors the narrative process through which various stories blend into each other just as the tears of two men in a theater produce an unexpected bridge between their lives. Otherwise disconnected sequences are linked by intertitles indicating the passage of time ("Several Months Later," "Three Weeks Later," "Four Years Earlier," "A Month Later," "Eight Months Later"). Two of these sequences ("Three Weeks Later" and "A Month Later") present flashbacks-within-flashbacks. Such temporal shufflings further blur the lines between seemingly discrete episodes of action and thereby lay the groundwork for the film's merging of identities.

As Almodóvar describes its structure, "*Talk to Her* tells an intimate, romantic, secret story, spiced with independent and spectacular sequences. I'm referring to the bullfights, the inclusion of 'The Shrinking Lover,' the sequence with Caetano Veloso in which he performs 'Cucurrucucú paloma,' Pina Bausch's choreography of 'Café Müller' and 'Masurca Fogo,' the dance pieces that begin and end the film" (*Hable*).

In and of themselves, none of these stories is complex. The interweaving structure and the quantity and range of embedded stories create the outward impression of complexity.

The title of the film, echoing Benigno's advice, also underscores storytelling as the self-conscious structural device through which characters communicate with each other. Almodóvar calls the film "a celebration of narration in itself" (Strauss, *Entretien* 196). It includes the narratives told through dance, the bullfighting scenes involving Lydia, the musical narrative of "Cucurrucucú paloma," and the storytelling activities of the two male protagonists. In Almodóvar's original conception of the film, the paired narrations of Marco and Benigno, "who tell the story of themselves to someone who cannot hear them" (Almodóvar, *Hable*), gave order to the larger narrative design of the film.

Almodóvar speaks of the essential element of "mystery" within the plotting of this and his next film, *Bad Education* (Strauss, *Entretien* 197), in both of which the audience is driven along with the characters to engage in the kind of interrogation and decipherment conventionally identified with detective work. We may see how this works in a scene in which disjunction and its psychological recuperation is apparent: the insertion of "Cucurrucucú paloma." The action is introduced as Marco sits vigil over Lydia. He stares out of the camera frame as if recalling something. We cut to a high-angle shot of an unidentified swimmer in a glistening aqua-blue swimming pool. The camera locates the source of the music: a gathering of people surrounding Veloso and his musicians. Then there is a slow tracking across the faces of his gathered audience seated in the patio of a country house. We may identify Marisa Paredes and Cecilia Roth, actresses who had appeared in *All about My Mother.* We also recognize Marco, moved to tears by the song. The lyrics tell the story of a lover's loss of his beloved. The motif of Marco's tears seems to refer back to the opening scene, where he was so moved by the ballet. Marco now walks off with Lydia and comments on the power of Veloso's rendition. In this manner, the song and surrounding scene appear to function as an autonomous musical interlude that punctuates action and could easily be eliminated.

Yet the song illuminates the action by illustrating it in a different context. The lyrics of the popular Mexican folk ballad emphasize tears ("no llores" [don't cry]) and include a reference to the return of a lost lover, echoing Marco's emotional state and providing a symbolic condensation of the larger narrative motif of lost loved ones. The song's emotional effect evokes a melodramatic element, although, in sharp distinction to the conventional treatment of melodramatic tears in film, the motif is now identified with male as opposed to female characters.

As this interlude illustrates, the storytelling process identified with Benigno and Marco is not as simple and straightforward as the film's linear plot might suggest. We see this in the case of Marco's narrow perspective in recounting crucial events on the day of Lydia's goring at the *corrida* in Córdoba. His narration is distinctive in that it is the only event in the film told twice. The first telling occurs at the beginning of the episode titled "Several Months Later." Marco and Lydia are in the backseat of a limousine as it moves through the Andalusian countryside. The scene begins with a close-up of their hands affectionately intertwined. Lydia speaks: "We have to talk tonight, after the bullfight," to which he responds: "But we've been talking for an hour." "You have," she retorts. In the sequence entitled "A Month Later," as Marco and Benigno stand over Alicia and Lydia on the terrace, Marco recalls that it has been two months to the day since Lydia was gored. The scene jumps to the interior of a small church as we witness the marriage ceremony of an unidentified young couple. We eventually locate Lydia crying in one of the pews. Marco is nearby and accompanies her outside the church. They get into the limousine, and he begins to tell her that he has gotten over his attachment to Angela, his former lover, after having been separated from her for ten years. The scene then picks up the dialogue that we had previously viewed regarding Lydia's insistence that they talk after the *corrida*. A narrative ellipsis brings us back to the present; we see Marco enter Lydia's room at the sanitarium and find El niño de Valencia, Lydia's former lover (Adolfo Fernández), at her bedside. In El niño's explanation of his presence, the enigma of the repeated scene is explained. Lydia's tears at the wedding were tears of happiness because she was planning to marry El niño; this is why she needed to talk to Marco after the bullfight. This complex though largely unobtrusive juxtaposition of scenes effectively masks the true nature of Marco's relationship with Lydia—it is marred by his self-absorption, which undercuts true communication. For him, as for his audience, the discovery that his relationship with Lydia was already over before the bullfight comes as a surprise.

In important ways, Marco's distorted storytelling of his relationship with Lydia prefigures the more central element of Benigno's sexual relation with Alicia, the revelation of which is constructed around the *Shrinking Lover* episode. This interlude, in which Benigno recounts to Alicia the plot of a silent film he has just seen at the Filmoteca, is the most complex of the stories and performances interpolated into the film. It is strategically integral to the framing story out of which it arises in ways that the Pina Bausch dances or the Caetano Veloso cameo are not. The film-within-the-film involves a series of characters in no way related to the stories of Marco or Benigno, and yet, as Almodóvar makes clear, this story is not only grounded in the narrative that frames it but is also related to that frame thematically and visually.

Almodóvar calls the seven-minute sequence a "detour" from the main story of the film, but it is used as *una tapadera* (a lid) to cover up what is really happening. *The Shrinking Lover* recasts the story of the union of the nurse and the comatose dancer into a version in which the woman, Amparo (Paz Vega), is a scientist. Her lover, Alfredo (Fele Martínez), impulsively drinks the experimental potion Amparo has prepared and begins to shrink. Amparo finally recovers him at his mother's house and steals him away in her purse to the Hotel Youkalli, an allusion to the Edenic space first introduced in *Kika*. In the surreal final scene of the film-within-the-film, we see Amparo asleep in bed under a sheet, an image that recalls Alicia lying comatose. The now diminutive Alfredo penetrates the vagina of his beloved in an act that is not only a narrative expression of lovemaking but also the male's return to the womb. The final high-angle shot of Amparo asleep in what appears to be a dream of sexual contentment is then "matched" with a parallel image of Alicia in her bed. Benigno's lovemaking with (or rape of) the comatose Alicia is thus metaphorically narrated through the silent-film plot that Benigno began recounting to her. It is not until later that the meaning of *The Shrinking Lover*, in the context of Benigno's relation to Alicia, is made clear.

Shot in black and white with camera work that simulates the visual-narrative style of silent-cinema classics (Almodóvar cites Murnau's

Sunrise [1928] as one of his inspirations), *The Shrinking Lover* is orchestrated with a score by Alberto Iglesias that provides an appropriately uncanny look and sound of period silent film. The quality of nonverbal communication between bodies becomes one of the important axes of narrative meaning in this sequence, as it does in the framing story within which the silent film is narrated. The insistence on the nonverbal subtly undercuts Benigno's advice, "Talk to her," as it suggests that images, especially those related to bodies, are more powerful than words.

Words become problematic precisely as they are seen as a deceptive subterfuge in the structure of *The Shrinking Lover.* As with the protagonist of Highsmith's *This Sweet Sickness,* Benigno is a deviant character who is normalized within the narrative by his seductive charm as a storyteller. Clearly, Alfredo's penetration of Amparo in the story-within-the-story coincides with and covers up Benigno's rape of Alicia. The silent film's play of scale with the images of the shrinking lover suggests Benigno's guilt in knowingly violating Alicia's body. While he is beguiling and childlike in his innocence, Javier Cámara's striking characterization underscores the sexual and moral ambiguity of Benigno's character. Only at fleeting moments do we get the sense that he is socially maladjusted. The female nurses make fun of him; Alicia's father, the psychiatrist he visits as a ruse to see where Alicia lives, suggests that he must have an emotional problem. After the rape, Benigno recalls that Alicia's father had even called him a psychopath.

By staging Alicia's rape through this process of cinematic "masking," Almodóvar problematizes Benigno's identity by a sleight of hand that brings the spectator to occupy the point of view of the rapist, who is also the storyteller. After a London screening at the National Film Theater, when asked why he engaged in such a "dangerous" narrative technique, Almodóvar responded: "'I did it to hide something that is going on in the film and something which the spectator should not see'" (qtd. in Mackenzie 157).

Beyond the question of morality, *The Shrinking Lover* emphasizes the power of the human body. The story underscores two fundamental conditions of the body that are in dialectical opposition throughout the film that frames it. One is the centrality of bodies in motion versus stasis, which is emphasized from beginning to end as a nonverbal mode of communication. From "Café Müller" to "Masurca Fogo," from Lydia's *corrida* to Alicia's dance practices, the performances of the body become ways to communicate with others. The idea of the body as the authentic instrument of narration ultimately holds the distinct parts of the film together.

The second and equally important element is that of confinement. In his review of the American premiere of *Talk to Her,* Elvis Mitchell wrote in the *New York Times:* "This is a movie about being trapped in various kinds of prisons, spiritual, physical, and finally literal." In this regard, Alicia and Lydia are versions of David in *Live Flesh,* the passionate individual trapped in a paralyzed body. At the same time, Benigno is painfully reminded throughout of the transparent barriers that separate him from his beloved. We see this in the repeated scenes of him longingly staring from the window of his apartment to the dance studio where Alicia rehearses. In the final stage of the plot, when he is incarcerated, we see him in the glass cubicle through which he can see and hear Marco, but cannot touch him. In their last conversation, his only wish is to be able to embrace Marco. Ultimately, the dramatic tension of the film is rooted in these seemingly opposite images of the body: of movement and of bodies constrained.

As Almodóvar comments on the theme of *Talk to Her:* "When the psychiatrist asks Benigno what his problem is, he responds: 'Loneliness, I suppose.' Marco says to the two women he is with in the film at distinct moments that he is lonely [*está solo*]. Marco and Benigno act without melodramatic flourish, simply stating the emptiness of their existence. Loneliness [*La soledad*] is something all the characters experience: Alicia and Lydia; Katerina, the dance teacher, Alicia's father. . . . 'Loneliness, I Suppose' is one of the possible titles for this film" (*Hable*).

Talk to Her won Almodóvar his second Oscar in as many years, this time for Best Screenplay. Notably, this was the first time since Claude Lelouche's *A Man and a Woman* (1964) and only the second time in academy history that a non-American film claimed that award. Almodóvar underplayed the significance of the second Oscar, arguing that the majority of Hollywood films are adaptations, and thus it is a less competitive award than it first appears (Strauss, *Entretien* 202). The award suggests, however, a critical vindication of the earlier years during which he had so defiantly fought the MPAA.

Bad Education (2004)

The origin of *Bad Education* dates back to an unpublished short story Almodóvar wrote in 1973. Over the years he returned to the script, eventually embellishing it with a complex time frame through which to interrogate the weight of history on a quasi-autobiographical character and, more broadly, to explore the appeal of the past as a contemporary nostalgic mode of film representation. In *Live Flesh,* he had created a brief historical sequence set in 1970 that frames and contextualizes the contemporary 1990s actions, but in *Bad Education* all the action is set in the past, focusing exclusively on three moments: 1980, 1977, and 1964. In this regard, we may consider this Almodóvar's first truly historical narrative.

Although the protagonist is not immediately recognizable as an obvious point of narrative identification for the spectator—he is a successful gay filmmaker involved in a highly individuated set of social and emotional circumstances—we gradually come to recognize his symbolic connection to a broader audience of Spaniards seduced by the nostalgic mode that old movies and popular culture of recent years have purveyed. Nostalgia becomes not only crucial to the narrative content of the film but also a strategy of audience address. The autobiographical dimension is further emphasized as Almodóvar conspicuously sets the framing situation of the film in 1980, the historical period of his first feature-length film, *Pepi, Luci, Bom, and Other Girls on the Heap.* The sense of the historical in that film was insistently assaulted, as the characters and director alike denied recognition of the weight of Spain's recent political past. In light of this self-referential interpolation of the director's earlier career, *Bad Education* invites us to view the implications of Almodóvar's reversal of the *pasotismo* of his previous anti-establishment filmmaking and to question a range of historical themes as they relate to individual and collective identity in contemporary Spain.

As with *Live Flesh,* the film's historical backstory is related to contemporary politics—specifically, the prominence of Spain's conservative Partido Popular (PP). The earlier film was made on the eve of the general elections that brought the PP to power in 1996. Ironically, *Bad Education* debuted in Madrid only days after the PP's fall from power in March 2004. Even without that symmetry, the political backstory of Almodóvar's fifteenth film would be relevant, since it implicates personal nostalgia in the formation of a contemporary political theme that gives historical resonance to characters and action.

Bad Education transcends a mere retro style, however, and becomes what Fredric Jameson calls "postNostalgia," a formal visual-narrative strategy that seeks to free its audience from the pull of pastness by developing a plot that works as a diagnostic apparatus through which to view and question the individual's relation to the representations of the past (287, 296). In this way the film constitutes a fundamental break from Almodóvar's earlier, less direct approaches to depicting the weight of Spanish history on his characters. The principal storyline concerns a filmmaker's nostalgia for a lost love, conveyed visually, in part, through cinematic self-references to past movie culture. That intimate story, paired with a series of cinematic quotes, parallels a less obvious back-story: the transformation of the ideologues of the old Francoist order of the 1960s into the new conservatives of the 1990s and beyond.

According to Almodóvar, the script went through some twenty different versions over the years, leading to a progressively more complex and ultimately broader vision of Spanish culture than is depicted in any of his previous films. Part of that complexity and expanded scope derives from the interplay of opposing cultural spaces: The contrasts between the traditionalist provinces (Valencia, Galicia) and culturally tolerant urban spaces (Madrid, Valencia) reflect the shifting social mores within Spain's evolving modernity. Yet Spanish urban and provincial spaces are not merely juxtaposed. Defying simple chronological or geographic order, the narrative jumps among these three locales and times, blurring the lines between the experiences of the past and a presumed contemporary moment. In this way, time and space are insistently marked by narrative fissures and discontinuities, self-consciously provoking audiences to question the narrative-historical flow constructed by the film. Unlike *Talk to Her*, in which different times and places are elided, the visual design of the narrative of *Bad Education* emphasizes the abrupt and often self-conscious leaps from past to present and from provincial to urban locales.

The complex plot of *Bad Education* focuses on Enrique Goded (Fele Martínez), a gay filmmaker who, while searching through newspaper

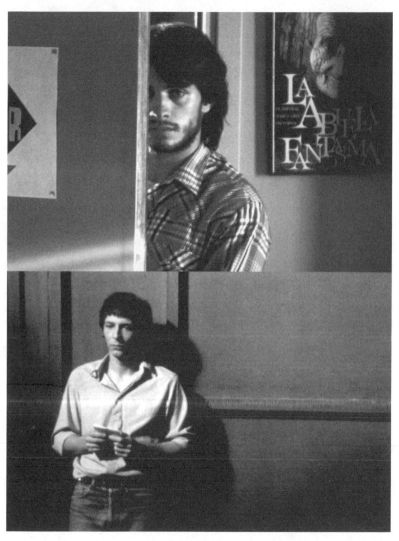

Gael García Bernal and Fele Martínez in
Bad Education. Courtesy of El Deseo S.A.

stories for inspiration for the script of his next film, receives a visit from a young man (Gael García Bernal) purporting to be Ignacio Rodríguez, a childhood friend. Ignacio is now an actor looking for a role in Enrique's next movie. Although they have not seen each other since childhood, Enrique is taken aback by Ignacio's appearance. He has trouble recognizing in him any physical resemblance to the young boy who was his first love in a religious school sixteen years earlier. Ignacio, who insists upon being called Angel Andrade, his new stage name, offers Enrique a short story he has written as a potential script, "La Visita" (The Visit), involving intimate details of their childhood experiences at the school.

As Enrique reads the story that night, he begins to visualize it as a film. The images, characters, and actions we see are his projection onto the mindscreen of his imagination. The first-person narration is conveyed through Ignacio's voiceover. "The Visit" is set on a fateful night in 1977 in a rural town in the province of Valencia, the same town where, years earlier, the two had studied. Ignacio is now a performer working under the stage name Zahara and appearing in a traveling drag show. Dressed as Sara Montiel, Ignacio lip-synchs songs by the Spanish superstar of the 1950s and 1960s. The morning after his performance, still dressed as Zahara, he visits the religious school planning to settle an old score with his former teacher, Father Manolo (Daniel Giménez Cacho). He has come to blackmail the priest who seduced him years earlier and who had expelled Enrique, his rival for Ignacio's affections, out of jealousy. Confronting the priest, Ignacio hands him a copy of the narrative of their sordid relations, which he threatens to sell to the newspapers if Father Manolo doesn't give him one million pesetas.

Intrigued by the cinematic possibilities of the story, Enrique agrees to adapt it into a film but is put off by his old friend's insistence on playing the part of Zahara. He tells Angel that he is too masculine for the role. They argue. After telling Enrique that there will be no film if he doesn't play Zahara, Angel leaves. In the following weeks, Enrique goes to the Galician village where Ignacio grew up to talk with Ignacio's mother. To his consternation, he learns that Ignacio has been dead for three years and discovers that the person who presented himself as Ignacio is really Juan, Ignacio's younger brother. After Enrique returns to Madrid, Angel reappears, having noticeably lost weight. He now offers Enrique the story for his film with no conditions, asking only that Enrique give him a screen test for the role of Zahara. Without mentioning that he knows he is really Juan, Enrique gives him the role, and the two men become lovers.

The production progresses with Juan playing the role of Zahara just as Enrique had envisioned it. On the day they shoot the final scene, Enrique's fictionalized version of Padre Manolo's murder of Zahara to cover up the scandal, a stranger appears on the set, a Mr. Berenguer (Lluís Homar), who turns out to be the former priest, now a successful executive who has come in search of Juan. Berenguer recounts to Enrique his version of the story of the two brothers. The adult Ignacio (Francisco Boira) reentered Berenguer's life in 1977, when the former choirboy was already a transvestite junkie in the process of having a sex change. He blackmailed Berenguer by threatening to expose his past identity as a pedophile priest. Through his renewed contact with his former victim, Berenguer met and became infatuated with Ignacio's younger brother Juan, who led the older man on for money and gifts in exchange for sexual favors. Meanwhile, Ignacio's desperation for money reached such a point that Berenguer felt he had no other choice but to kill him. Juan was also implicated in the murder for having given his brother a fatal dose of pure heroin. After hearing Berenguer's story, Enrique throws Juan out of his house, literally closing the door on him.

As Almodóvar details the thirty-year gestation of *Bad Education*, he notes that the final version of the script was built around three different "visitas," the word ambiguously meaning both the act of the visit and the vistor. They include Zahara's visit to Padre Manolo in Ignacio's story (the original visit that was the kernel of the film's conception); Juan's visit to Enrique's film production company El Azar in 1980, when, as the imposter Ignacio, he presents himself as Enrique's childhood friend and offers him "The Visit" as a potential script; and finally, Mr. Berenguer's visit to the set of Enrique's film, where the former priest witnesses a fictionalized version of his murder of Ignacio-Zahara that triggers his own retelling of the "true story" of Ignacio's death.

The plotting of the three encounters is guided by an inexorable narrative and visual logic from beginning to end. The opening credits start with the production company name, El Deseo (Desire), and introduce a series of radically juxtaposed images from the story to be unfolded as film, eventually connecting to the image of the door in the Madrid offices of "El Azar" through which Juan will intrude on Enrique's life. Therein begins a complex weaving of retrospective narrative threads that eventually leads to the final narrative gesture of the film, Enrique's closing of another door on which is emblazoned the word "Passion," as the director throws Juan out of his house and, presumably, his life.

The logic that connects the three visits, and moves us from "desire" to "passion," is the causality of cinematic plotting, as Almodóvar makes clear in his preface to the script (*Guión cinematográfico* 12–13). Yet that causal logic is broken up with a series of "gaps," time-jumps that are the result of the overlapping and, at times, simultaneous readings of the past by different characters. Inspired by the narrative formulas of flashback storytelling in Hollywood films noir, these overlapping and discontinuous narrations break up the viewer's sense of a sustained narrative chronology and thereby give special meaning to Almodóvar's choice of the name "El Azar" (chance) for Enrique's film production company. Ironically, for a film that represents Almodóvar's first "historical narrative," in which all action is set in the clearly labeled "historical" past, historical representation itself seems under continual seige by the film's enunciative apparatus.

This narrative strategy of "seige" is expressed in the credit sequence, in which we see the violent convergence of images and text intersecting each other, juxtaposing moments from different time periods in a visual and auditory style clearly reminiscent of the Bernard Hermann–Saul Bass collaborations for the credit sequences of Hitchcock's late 1950s and early 1960s thrillers. Those credits present in microcosm the process of narration of the cinematic story of *Bad Education*. In the ensuing film, time is insistently "cut up" and pasted through an array of graphic techniques: the narrowing of the screen frame to denote the past; the splitting of the image of Ignacio's face as Enrique and Padre Manolo read of the latter's sexual attack on Ignacio; freeze-framing certain images; the morphing of the faces of characters from past to present, all accompanied by a score that, as critics have suggested, appears to be an homage to the Hitchcock thriller. Such elements are at the service of a singular textual project: the effort to reframe a personal narrative as Spanish cultural history. It is that clash between cinematic narrative and history that the film explores—the collective experience of pastness and the personal experience of memory linked to images.

Of special note in this context is the way in which Almodóvar integrates a series of aural and visual allusions to the past as a form of address to the audience throughout the film. One of the most conspicuous of these is the scene of class recess at the religious school where the young boys and the priests play soccer. The image of a priest serving as goalie, shot from behind the goal net, is presented in freeze-frame to give the impression of the priest levitating. The frozen image recalls a widely circulated photograph by the famed Spanish photographer Ramón Masats, "Partit de Fútbol" (Soccer Match; 1960). This brief textual pause invites the Spanish audience of a certain age to acknowledge their own relation to the seductive images and sounds that long masked the predatory culture of Francoism that had formed and deformed them. Some of the visual complexity of *Bad Education* derives from the narrational process of moments such as this one in which the elements of popular culture of the Franco years prod the Spanish spectator's cultural memory as they evoke the period ambience of the plot.

In tandem with this visual complexity as it engages audiences in the scrutiny of their historical culture, the narration further destabilizes simplistic conceptions of history by contextualizing Ignacio's story from opposing narrative and emotional perspectives, those of the victim and the victimizer. Berenguer's version, told from the historical moment of 1980, picks up where Ignacio's story leaves off: It describes the former priest's willingness to be blackmailed by Ignacio in order to be close to his new prey, Juan. In this version, Berenguer represents himself as the victim of the two unscrupulous brothers. Through these narrational shifts, the notion of victimhood becomes fluid, variously attributed to Ignacio and Berenguer by virtue of the respective narrative points of view. Complicating the audience's understanding of the real Ignacio's narrative, "The Visit," is the fact that it is first told from Enrique's point of view as he reads Ignacio's story in 1980, a perspective that further reinforces the post-Franco notion of the ecclesiastical establishment as the true victimizers.

There is an essential difference between the two tellings: The script Enrique reads and embellishes is really a historical evocation of the repressive Francoist past. Evoking the critical year 1964, this is a story of corrupt ecclesiastical power, sexual transgression, and cover-up. Tellingly, Berenguer's story is set in a hedonistic post-Franco world of 1977 and is characterized by a matter-of-fact treatment of drugs and sex. These twin narratives use the storytelling process to reimagine history from opposing personal and cultural vantages. In this weave of stories and counterstories, each of the four protagonists, Enrique, Ignacio, Juan, and Berenguer, renegotiates the past as a way of forging his own contemporary identity. Viewed as a single cinematic plot, the perspectival play of events throws into question the meaning of that recent history, as it holds the key to contemporary identity construction. The film's narrative tension is transformed from an interrogation of history to the questioning of the modes and motives of each character in his depiction of the past.

Almodóvar describes the plot of *Bad Education* as a variation of Scheherezade's *Arabian Nights* (Strauss, *Entretien* 196), within which, as in the original, the framing situation is reflected in the stories narrated. At the center is Enrique Goded, the storyteller as filmmaker, who willfully vampirizes the events surrounding his first childhood love for the sake of making a movie. Ignacio has also vampirized his own life by writing "The Visit." As Almodóvar observes, each creator's motivation always exceeds the simple desire to create. Ignacio has written the story to blackmail Father Manolo; Enrique agrees to make the film egged on by the desire to find out about Ignacio's death and the real identity of Juan, the imposter Ignacio (Strauss, *Entretien* 198).

Enrique's motivation in knowingly submitting to Juan's deception is explained in a scene when, while cutting out curious *faits divers* from the newspapers in search of material for his script, he comes across a macabre news item about a woman who jumped into a crocodile pit at a Taiwanese zoo. As the crocodiles devoured her, she embraced one of them without ever screaming. Enrique's perverse motivation in knowingly accepting the situation in which he is manipulated by Juan thus appears to be an almost suicidal desire to know the source of Juan's enigmatic being and the true circumstances of Ignacio's death.

Embedded in the interwoven narratives is a singular image that crystallizes the underlying problematic of the film as a charged interrogation of the past. In this ambiguously situated scene, as Enrique reads "The Visit," the voiceover of Ignacio as a child speaks of Father Manolo's trips with his favorite boys to a rustic campsite. While the other boys swim, Manolo plays a guitar as Ignacio sings "Moon River." In the middle of the open-air rehearsal, we do not see the priest's attempt to molest Ignacio but hear the child's protesting voice and then see Ignacio jump away from the tree where they were seated. In his effort to flee from the priest, Ignacio falls to the ground. A close-up of the boy's stunned face reveals that he has cut his forehead in the fall. A crimson line of blood trickles down, abruptly splitting the screen and dividing Ignacio's face into two half-images in freeze-frame. The image next cuts to a close-up of Father Manolo in 1977 as he reads Ignacio's story, followed by a cut to a parallel image of Enrique completely absorbed in the story of Zahara's visit to the priest from the vantage of 1980.

This doubling of the "reading present" emphasizes the emotional lure and dramatic impact of the past on the characters. The staging of this story-within-the-story, involving representations of three historical moments, also serves to blur the lines separating past and present for characters and audience alike. The splitting of Enrique's mindscreen comes to signify a gap, a point of textual interrogation out of which comes Enrique's perverse investigation of Ignacio's death and the revelation of Juan's true identity as the imposter Ignacio. The splitting of the image of Ignacio's face is motivated by the child Ignacio's words from the story Enrique is reading: "A thread of blood split my face in two. I had a sense of foreboding that the same thing would happen to my life: it would always be split in two and there would be no way to avoid that."

That bifurcation permeates the film's treatment of history and personal memory. We see this in the elaborate chiaroscuro that orders the mise-en-scène throughout. The somber and shadowy depictions of Madrid in 1980 and Valencia in 1977 frame a third time and place: the seemingly Edenic childhood space of innocent first love in 1964. We are in an idealized provincial locale, marked by the radiant natural light of the outdoors and its antithesis, the shadowy confines of a religious boarding school. Importantly, from the present-day vantage of Enrique's Madrid of 1980, this past is evoked through auditory as well as visual imagination. The dominant features of that past include the voices of a boys' religious choir and of Ignacio singing versions of "Torna a Sorrento" and "Moon River." Sounds merge with images through the soundtrack voice of Sara Montiel in Mario Camus's *Esa mujer* (That Woman), a film Enrique recalls that he and Ignacio saw together. In the dark interior of the local movie theater, away from the vigilance of the priests, under the flickering light shed by the screen, the two young boys masturbated each other.

To some degree, the year 1964 seems an arbitrary choice of time frame in which to situate the pivotal action that shaped all subsequent events. *Esa mujer* was not even made until 1969. We need to see beyond this minor anachronism, however, to discern Almodóvar's effort to underscore the characters' paradigmatic coming to awareness and, more symbolically, that of Spanish cinema itself. As he explains in an interview: "'The year of the picture [*Esa mujer*] is 1964, the same year as *El extraño viaje* [The Strange Journey] by Fernán-Gómez, the same year as *La tía Tula* [*Aunt Tula;* Miguel Picazo]. I know a lot about that closed world, of mourning and religiosity that prevented us from living. It's not that way now, they can't control our lives and prevent us from living them'" (qtd. in Rioyo 30).

Cinematic quotations provide a key to the development of nearly all aspects of the film, particularly in the case of Juan. As with Benigno in *Talk to Her,* the character of Juan traces his genealogy to a Patricia Highsmith novel, *The Talented Mister Ripley,* but filtered through a cinematic source, René Clérment's 1960 French adaptation of the novel, in which a young Alain Delon played Highsmith's perverse title character: "Juan has a beautiful face, which doesn't allow anyone to guess his true nature. Evil is never apparent in Patricia Highsmith's novels. Her killers know very well how to blend into society, and only their victims recognize them. Juan is on the amoral side of Highsmith's characters, those who are elusive and, what is more, who represent the classic figure of film noir, the femme fatale" (Strauss, *Entretien* 190). Tellingly, in the final sequence of *Bad Education,* after the completion of Enrique's film, García Bernal's face appears physically to have been made over to look like that of the young Delon of the Clérmont film.

Almodóvar defines the femme fatale as "a woman conscious of the power of seduction, cold-blooded, which means she doesn't falter easily; she's lost all scruples and she's not interested in recovering them. For her, sex is not a source of pleasure but rather for inflicting pain on others. In *Bad Education* the femme fatale is an 'enfant terrible' played by Gael

García Bernal, who follows in the footsteps of Barbara Stanwyck, Jane Greer, Jean Simmons [*Angel Face*], Joan Bennet [*Scarlet Street*], Ann Dvorak, Mary Winsor, Lizbeth Scott, Veronica Lake, and other curses in the form of women" (*La mala educación*).

In this refiguring of the classic film-noir femme fatale, Almodóvar joins genre film quotes to gender refiguration and the idea of creativity as emblemized in the character's willful self-construction. We have seen variations of this cluster of elements in Femme Letal in *High Heels* and also in Agrado in *All about My Mother*. In one regard, the measure of Juan's malevolence is reflected in his having vampirized his own brother's identity, which produces the vertiginous *regressus in infinitum* within which the younger brother's ambition to become a successful actor leads him to embrace the improbable role of Zahara, mirroring the real Ignacio's desire to be a woman fashioned after Sara Montiel, the kitsch icon of 1960s Spanish gay culture. Almodóvar says of Montiel: "'She . . . was a pop icon of the 'homos' and the cross-dressers. She was a star in the style of Mae West and Marlene Dietrich, a personality, a way of being in front of the camera that made her different from all the other stars'" (qtd. in Rioyo 34).

Within the narrative, creativity is identified with the image of Sara Montiel. Montiel enters the text as pure invention. The adult Ignacio, the writer of the story, projects his desire to be a woman onto the fantastic body of Montiel. Enrique's imaging of Ignacio's story has Montiel as a blonde despite the fact that she almost always appeared as black-haired or brunette in her films. Enrique's version seems more inspired by the cinematic references of sexualized blondes from American film noir. The scene in which Enrique visualizes Zahara lip-synching a Montiel song, "Quizás" (Perhaps), bears a striking similarity to the "Recordarás" performance by Femme Letal in *High Heels*, as it too evokes a past that speaks to Enrique and, finally, Padre Manolo as well.

To some degree, these film quotes follow a pattern already noted in earlier films: Characters go to the movies to see their future, not their past (*Splendor in the Grass, Duel in the Sun, All about Eve*). In the 1964 sequence, Almodóvar shows Enrique and Ignacio viewing the moment in *Esa mujer* in which Montiel returns to the convent where she had been a nun. The Mother Superior does not recognize her and tells her she should not be there. The scene foreshadows the events to come in

"The Visit." Later, after Juan and Berenguer have poisoned Ignacio, they kill time by going to a noir double-feature: Renoir's *La Bête Humaine* and Marcel Carné's *Therese Raquin,* stories that mirror their situation, thus leading Berenguer to lament as they leave the theater, "It's as if the movies were talking about us."

Adding to this noir mirroring are two other important cinematic citations that structure the action: Billy Wilder's *Double Indemnity,* which provides the model for Juan's manipulation of Berenguer, and Hitchcock's *Vertigo.* Berenguer's telling of his reencounter with Ignacio in Valencia and his plotting of Ignacio's murder with Juan makes marked overtures to the plot of the Wilder film, which in Spanish was appropriately called *Perdición.* Almodóvar shoots Juan in sunglasses strolling through the Museo de Gigantes y Cabezudos (Museum of Giant Masks), fashioned after the scene in *Double Indemnity* in which Barbara Stanwyck and Fred MacMurry stroll down a supermarket aisle, planning details of the murder of Stanwyck's husband. *Vertigo* is the overarching intertext of the entire film, providing a model for the plotline of Juan's triple role as himself, the imposter version of his brother, and the drag queen Zahara in Ignacio's story. As with Hitchcock's development of the dual roles performed by Kim Novak in *Vertigo,* the imposture is designed to deceive not only the fictional protagonist but the audience as well.

The most notable dimension of this creative recycling of films is Almodóvar's own self-vampirization by recycling with significant modification parts of *Law of Desire.* In his "self-interview" for *Bad Education,* he acknowledges an obvious connection between the two films. In the earlier film, the transsexual Carmen Maura enters the chapel of the religious school where she studied as a young boy. There she meets Padre Constantino, the priest who seduced her as a child. According to Almodóvar, the sequence has a common genealogy with *Bad Education* in the original story of "The Visit" (*La mala educación*).

More than in any of Almodóvar's previous films, explicit and oblique cinematic quotations create a critical distance for his spectators between a dramatized present and a highly distorted past. The complex historicized narrative of *Bad Education* leads to an alignment of that critical distance around the film's political theme, embodied in the double-faced presence of Manolo/Berenguer. For Spanish audiences, especially those of Almodóvar's generation, the Father Manolo of the early sequences is a familiar figure from the old Spanish cultural imaginary: the predatory nature of Francoist culture so closely aligned to the Catholic church, its hypocrisy and violence worked out on the innocent minds of children. Ironically, Almodóvar tells an interviewer, "the priest is probably my favorite character in *Bad Education*" (Hirschberg 27).

With the advent of democracy came the assumed extinction of the specters of Francoism. As the prologue to *Live Flesh* shows, however, demons of the past survive in new forms. *Bad Education* shapes its historical reflexivity out of the thematics of recycled monsters. The demon has changed his appearance: He is no longer the old priest bugger Father Manolo but the suave Mr. Berenguer, literary editor of a Valencian publishing house interested in the works of promising young writers. That is how he comes back into contact with Ignacio. The predatory villains of Francoism may have altered their appearance and name, but their objective remains unchanged. At the same time, the film poses the destructive attraction of the past for the characters as pointedly dramatized in Enrique's double bind: his effort to recuperate the memory of Ignacio, an irretrievable, innocent first love, and his involuntary engagement with Juan, the imposter Ignacio who embodies the falsification and exploitation of that past. Thus, while the story may be read as the

Almodóvar directing young actors in
Bad Education. Courtesy of El Deseo S.A.

self-vampirization of the artist's life or the impossibility of a return to the past, its expansive historical frame and the multiple identities of its characters make it also an allegory of the problematic persistence of Old Spain in its varied disguises. It is in this context, finally, that the narrative labyrinth that Almodóvar constructs aligns the stories of individual impostures with the false and politically dangerous nostalgia for a collective Spanish past.

On the eve of the Spanish debut of *Bad Education,* Almodóvar found himself again confronting the demons of the old order in a political skirmish with the Partido Popular. The film had already achieved a unique historical status by being the first Spanish film ever invited to inaugurate the Cannes Film Festival, and it was scheduled to open in Spain two days after the general elections. Three days before the elections, on March 11, 2004, a series of terrible bombings shook Madrid's Atocha train station and two nearby suburban stations, killing 191 people. Spokesmen for the conservative government of José María Aznar claimed the bombings were the work of the Basque Terrorist group ETA (Euskadi ta Askatasuna), downplaying the argument that the attack was the work of al Qaeda to avenge Aznar's support of George W. Bush's invasion of Iraq. There were massive street demonstrations in Madrid and other Spanish cities, as Spaniards demanded information from the government before they went to vote. Rumors spread that the government was planning to postpone the elections. At a press conference for *Bad Education,* Almodóvar echoed these rumors. His televised statements were taken by the Aznar administration as a direct accusation against them as plotters of a presumed preelection coup. They threatened to have Almodóvar jailed. He spent the next month receiving threats from far-right extremists.

The political firestorm that accompanied the Spanish release of *Bad Education* seemed to vindicate the film's political thematics. The "bad education" of the title, in this regard, refers not only to the remembrance of formal schooling but to more pervasive cultural processes that continue to act upon the contemporary Spanish psyche. Never fully repudiated within the culture of the Transition, the past has returned, as Almodóvar suggests, in the form of new demons. In constructing this, his most accomplished script, he has turned his and Spain's obsession with the past into a political allegory of the susceptibility to false nostalgia.

We may read *Bad Education* as a self-conscious acknowledgment by Almodóvar of where he was in 1980 and how, through the evolution of a style and a conception of filmmaking, he has moved to a critique of his own past and the culture out of which his cinema has taken shape. With no small irony, therefore, he has situated the center of the plot of *Bad Education* in the suggestively autobiographical Madrid of 1980, the very year and place of the premiere of his first commercial feature.

Interview with Pedro Almodóvar |

Pleasure and the New Spanish Mentality

MARSHA KINDER. What do you think is the primary appeal of your films, especially *Law of Desire,* which has had such international success, whereas most Spanish films have had such difficulty in getting international distribution?

PEDRO ALMODÓVAR: Well, I've been striving for this over the last three years, and I think this is the fruit of my previous work. People know me more now, and it's easier for me to sell a film. On the other hand, I think my films are very contemporary. They represent more than others, I suppose, the New Spain, this kind of new mentality that appears in Spain after Franco dies, especially after 1977 till now. Stories about the New Spain have appeared in the mass media of every country. Everybody has heard that now everything is different in Spain, that it has changed a lot, but it is not so easy to find this change in the Spanish cinema. I think in my films they see how Spain has changed, above all, because now it is possible to do this kind of film here. Not that a film like *Law of Desire* would be impossible to make in places like Germany, London, or the United States.

MK: Yes, but it would be impossible to have such a film get half of its financing from the Ministry of Culture in any of those countries! How would you define "the new Spanish mentality"?

PA: I believe that the new Spanish mentality is less dramatic—although I demonstrate the contrary in my films. We have consciously left behind many prejudices, and we have humanized our problems. We have lost the fear of earthly power (the police) and of celestial power (the church), and we have also lost our provincial certainty that we are superior to the rest of the world—that typical Latin prepotency. And we have recuperated the inclination toward sensuality, something typically Mediterranean. We have become more skeptical, without losing the joy of living. We don't have confidence in the future, but we are constructing a past for ourselves because we don't like the one we had.

MK: Do you think that the appeal of your films also has something to do with their unique tone? I know that Pauline Kael in her very enthusiastic review of *Law of Desire* stressed the uniqueness of the tone without really describing what it is.

PA: Well, I would like to think this is one of the reasons because this is the main difference of my films. Whether they are good or bad, my films are absolutely different from other Spanish films and even from the other foreign cinema. I mean, you can talk about a lot of influences, everybody has them. But if you see all of my films, I'm sure you can differentiate them from the others, you can recognize them. I would like to think this is the main reason for their international appeal.

MK: How would you define that tone?

PA: It's hard for me to talk about it because I never try to verbalize about my films, but it's true there is a different tone, even in general. This is something I'm obsessed with when I'm working with the actors. They have to say my lines in a different way. Even for me this is something that's very difficult to explain to them because you have to catch it and you have to feel it. When I'm shooting, I'm obsessed with creating an atmosphere that explains exactly what is my tone. The atmosphere that I create when I'm shooting, this is the tone of my films. To take one example, I used to mix all the genres. You can say my films are melodramas, tragicomedies, comedies, or whatever, because I used to put everything together and even change genre within the same sequence and very quickly. But the main difference is the private morality. I think one auteur is different from another because he has his own morality. When I say morality, I don't mean ethics, it's just a private point of view. I mean, you can see a film by Luis Buñuel, and you know exactly that it belongs to Buñuel because it's just the way of thinking.

MK: It seems to me that what lies at the center of your unique tone is what you were describing before, that fluidity with which you move so quickly from one genre to another, or from one feeling or tone to another, so that when a line is delivered, it's very funny and borders on parody, and we spectators are just ready to laugh, but at the same time it's erotic and moves us emotionally. In this way, you always *demonstrate* that you're in control, that you're manipulating the spectator response.

PA: Yes, it takes more care than other styles of acting and shooting. You have to be very careful to control the tone because it can easily run away with you and go too far. Just as you say, in my films everything is just at the border of parody. It's not only parody. It's also the borderline of the ridiculous and of the grotesque. But it's easy to fall over the line.

MK: Other filmmakers who come to mind as doing something similar with tone are David Lynch . . .

PA: Absolutely, I recognize myself a lot in *Blue Velvet*. I love it.

MK: I love that film, too. It allows you to be both terrified and turned on, and at the same time it's also hysterically funny. And then there's Fassbinder.

PA: But the difference is that Fassbinder, as a German, doesn't have much of a sense of humor. In *Blue Velvet* you can find a great sense of humor, but *Blue Velvet* is more morbid than my films because there is always an element of naïveté in what I'm doing. It's strangely antithetical because I'm not so naïve. But this kind of purity of actions, feelings, and spontaneity, that's not in *Blue Velvet*. *Blue Velvet* is darker, sicker, sick in every way. But with a lot of humor. Do you think there is humor in Fassbinder's films?

MK: Oh yes, although it's always combined with pain.

PA: German culture is so different from Spanish culture. In our culture there is a great sense of humor, but not in the German culture. Also, I believe that our culture is more visceral. Intuition and imagination influence us more than reason. There is more adventure and spontaneity. We don't fear disorder or chaos.

MK: Your use of Hollywood melodrama—especially in *What Have I Done to Deserve This?* where two characters go to see *Splendor in the Grass,* and in *Matador,* where there's a long excerpt from *Duel in the Sun*—it seems similar to the ways in which Fassbinder used *Sirk* and even Billy Wilder's *Sunset Boulevard* in *Veronika Voss,* where he picked something already very extreme and then pushed it even further to that borderline of parody. How do you see the relationship between your work and Hollywood melodrama?

PA: All of the influences on me and all of the film references in my films are very spontaneous and visual. I don't make any tributes. I'm a very naïve spectator. I can't learn from the movies that I love. But if I had to choose one master or model, I would choose Billy Wilder. He represents exactly what I want to do.

MK: Which Billy Wilder? His films are so varied!

PA: Both Billy Wilders. The *Sunset Boulevard* Billy Wilder and *The Apartment* Billy Wilder, the *1-2-3* and *The Lost Weekend. The Lost Weekend,* for example, is a big, big drama, but you can find a lot of humor in it and a lot of imagination in the way it develops a unique situation. It's a great challenge for a screenwriter. But to return to the question of Hollywood, I just love that big period of the classic American melodrama. I'm not just talking about Sirk but about the kinds of films Bette Davis made. I like these extreme genres where you can talk naturally about strong sentiments without a sense of the ridiculous. This is something that melodrama has. But, of course, all these films like *Splendor in the Grass* and *Duel in the Sun,* which is so outrageous, I mean, you have to be very very brave to dare to go to this kind of extreme, you can really be grotesque if you don't know how to do it. This is something that I like. But I use the genre in a different way. My films are not so conventional as that kind of melodrama. Because I don't respect the boundaries of the genre, I mix it with other things. So my films appear to be influenced by Hollywood melodrama, but I put in other elements that belong more to my culture. For example, *What Have I Done to Deserve This?* is more like a neorealist film than melodrama. I think it's more like the films of Rossellini, Zavattini, and DeSica—more like Italian neorealism, which is also a melodramatic genre. But I put in a lot of humor. That makes the reality even more awful in a way, more extreme. And I also put in a lot of surrealistic elements that completely change the genre. I think that the presence of the nonrational in my films is strong, but I never try to explain it. For example, in *What Have I Done?* I don't try to explain the girl with the telekinetic powers, the girl like Carrie. I just put her in as part of the life or plot, and this kind of element changes the genre.

MK: There's a moment in *What Have I Done?* that helps me understand what you might mean by calling it a neorealist film. In one scene, the older son asks for help with his homework in assigning the labels "realist" and "romantic" to famous authors, and his granny reverses the traditional answers, calling Byron a realist and Balzac a romantic. Isn't this joke a comment on your own style? Isn't this exactly what you're doing in this movie—reversing the traditional meanings of realist and romantic?

PA: That could be, but I had no consciousness of it.

MK: In one of your interviews, you say you admired very much the Spanish neorealism of Marco Ferreri and Fernando Fernán-Gómez, films like *El pisito* (The Little Flat; 1958), *El cochecito* (The Little Car; 1960), and *La vida por delante* (Life Awaits You; 1958)—films that combined neorealism with a Spanish absurdist black humor called *esperpento*. In his new book *Out of the Past*, John Hopewell says that *What Have I Done?* continues in this tradition. Is this connection valid?

PA: Yes, very much so. If you have to find some source or relation to Spanish movies for my films, I think they are related to that kind of film. And also to an early film by Francisco Regueiro, *Duerme, Duerme, Mi Amor* (Sleep, Sleep, My Love; 1974). It's wonderful. Have you seen that film?

MK: Yes, it's desperately funny, and I can definitely see the connections with the absurdist black humor and the high-rise living theme in *What Have I Done?*

PA: Yes, this is one line I admire very much, and also early Berlanga. For me, Berlanga's *Plácido* (1961) is a model.

MK: Is it the film's rapid pacing and its ensemble of comic characters that appeal to you?

PA: Yes, and also this kind of tragic situation, very dark and very sad, but with great naturalness, and this kind of comedy that talks about a lot of things in life very seriously, and this kind of confusion of a lot of people all talking and doing different things at the same time. ·

MK: Yes, I can see those qualities in your films, especially in *What Have I Done?* . . . I think one of the most amazing things about *What Have I Done?* is that whereas it starts out with distanced reflexivity (with Carmen Maura walking past a film crew as she goes to work as a maid in a martial arts gym) and with burlesque (when she mimics their sword moves with her broom and has a torrid sexual encounter with a man in a shower who proves to be impotent), still amidst all of the satiric absurdities Maura's performance miraculously remains so realistic that she still manages to generate emotional identification in the spectator. And this has a big payoff in the final sequence when she is saved from suicide by the homecoming of her homosexual son who has just walked out on the lecherous dentist his mother left him with in order to cover the dental bill. We still get a big emotional rush from their reunion, and we're marveling, how did Almodóvar manage to pull this off?

PA: Yes, I tried to do that. This is always the challenge that I face whenever I make a film. . . . I try to solve the problem of how to get the big emotion from the audience, how to get emotional identification with the problem (in this case, high-rise apartment living), which lies behind the façade of absurdity, because everything just under the façade is absolutely real. And I think the audience can always recognize very clearly what I'm trying to say about life in the high-rise. And the jokes have many reasons for being there. For example, the opening titles sequence is very much like an abstract or experimental film with all the crew there making a film while the female protagonist goes to work in that place. That was the square where we were shooting; it was very direct. And in the gym where they're doing kendo, it looks like parody, but it also shows a very aggressive sport—one that releases aggression. And from the beginning you see that she's going to be in a male world and that males are the violent, strong ones who do this kind of thing. And she is just cleaning up. And then she tries to imitate them, just to be more quiet.

MK: It also prepares for her killing her husband with an ox bone.

PA: It's just the surface that's surrealistic, but I think you can understand very well what's just behind that surface. But I always try to work with all of these elements and to make it so that the people can feel it. Another example is the big confession scene in *The Law of Desire* when Carmen Maura, as Tina the transsexual, is trying to tell her brother Pablo about her relationship with their father. You know this is really hard. It's very strange, it's not easy to find a girl like that. Well, but I hope, and I felt that during this speech the audience really identifies with Tina as if she were the girl next door, someone with whom they can readily identify. I mean, this is really *heavy*. She committed incest, and she changed her sex to be with her father. She's one in a million. In this case, the acting is very important. It's Carmen Maura. If she hadn't been so perfect, then you never could have believed it. To do this kind of thing, you have to be very very careful. But if you succeed with that, then the audience can believe and understand everything.

MK: Even within that scene, you seem to purposely make it even harder for yourself, I mean in the way you set it up with her brother's amnesia, which is a highly contrived and corny way of motivating why Tina has to tell him and the audience about her past at this particular moment. And then that comical touch when she mentions Madrid, and then points out the window, saying, Oh yes, this is Madrid! reminding herself and us of the amnesia. And even with these absurdities, we are still swept away by Maura's performance.

PA: Yes, in that scene even Carmen was very surprised because she told me that when I was directing her, I asked her to do exactly the opposite of what she thought was right for this scene. She was sure that everyone else would have asked her to do exactly the contrary of what I said. Because the confession was very quiet, not very dramatic. So perhaps that's why you can believe it better, I don't know.

MK: There seems to be a movement in *Law of Desire* that is parallel to the one in *What Have I Done?* where you start with reflexivity, in this case a film-within-a-film, in which someone dictates from a script how a young man is to masturbate, and a voyeuristic spectator who . . .

PA: Imitates what he sees, yes . . .

MK: In a way, you start out by demystifying how movies work, but then by the end of the film those same dynamics still work on the audience very powerfully. A filmmaker like Buñuel, in showing you how it happens, prevents you from experiencing that kind of pleasure—he offers you a *different* kind of pleasure. But you demonstrate how the pleasure works and then make the spectator experience it despite the demonstration.

PA: Yes, that's true.

MK: My favorite moment in *Law of Desire* is when all the people at the end—Tina, the little girl Ada, and the police—look up with wonder at the window of the apartment where Pablo and his murderous lover Antonio are having their final hour of passionate love.

PA: Yes, this is one of the moments I'm proudest of—it's like a ritual with the music. I told the cinematographer [Ángel Luis Fernández], make it surprising and magical—not exactly like real magic, but like that moment when everyone looks up at the UFOs in *Close Encounters of the Third Kind.* I like it very much.

MK: It's wonderful. Their faces are full of awe and envy. Even the police are softened and eroticized by the passion they imagine is going on inside that room. They become the quintessential Almodóvar spectators! Isn't this the third time such a spectatorial moment occurs in the film? The first is the opening where Antonio is watching and is turned on by the erotic scene from Pablo's movie. And the second occurs in the middle of the film where Tina asks a man in the street to hose her down while her brother Pablo and the child Ada watch in wonder. Isn't the film's structure controlled by these three spectatorial moments?

PA: Yes, all three moments you have mentioned are the key to the film. The beginning is the key to understanding everything. I try to put the spectator into the field that I'm going to explore—the field of desire. Everyone understands that you can pay someone to make love to you. But it's very difficult to recognize that you can pay someone just to *listen* to your desire, which is something very different. This sensual desire is more abstract. It's just the necessity of feeling desire in an absolute way. This is the problem in the film. And also, as you said, I explain how the movie is made. You see just the interior of the movie. But also I explain the director's behavior—the relationship between director and actor. The director, on the one hand, is a voyeur, but he also is pushing, dictating exactly what he wants to be enacted, he wants to be represented, and this is very important to the relationship of power and voyeurism between the director and the actor.

MK: And yet aren't both being controlled by the script, which is probably why the script and the typewriter become so essential in the film—with all those huge close-ups and expressionistic angles of the keyboard? I read in one interview where you say the force of Pablo's imagination is stronger than his feelings, and that's why he takes the vengeance on the typewriter—why he throws the typewriter out the window at the end. But couldn't you also say that the script links Pablo to patriarchal discourse?

PA: I don't understand.

MK: Isn't Pablo like his father—a seducer who prefers young boys and who's never totally committed? Doesn't he reenact his father's seduction of his brother and also inspire his lovers to make a sacrifice? Pablo may want to be in control, but isn't he as shaped by his father as Tina was? Aren't his scripts and movies vehicles for patriarchal ideology?

PA: Well, I didn't think of that. Those are new ideas to me, but I agree with them and find them interesting. I like to discover new explanations in my films. It makes them richer. The opening is the main sequence of desire, of abstract desire rather than of sensual pleasure. Sensuality and physical pleasure are far better represented in the central sequence where Tina says, "Hose me!" than in the opening where the boy says, "Fuck me!" That's an important distinction in the film.

MK: But isn't there submission in both? Aren't they both part of the same masochistic aesthetic that also leads you to put the lust-in-the-dust ending of *Duel in the Sun* in the middle of *Matador?*

PA: I don't see it as masochism. Masochism requires pain, and I don't find it in my films. . . . I don't see masochism even in the Carmen Maura figure Tina, who is so obsessed with her past. She doesn't want to forget anything, even her worst memories. She's very engaged with her worst memories, they even feed her. This can be masochism too . . . a kind of quotidian masochism. In life in general you have to accept pain. It's a kind of adventure, and sometimes pain is the price you have to pay; the things you get are more important than the pain. But masochism requires that you *like* to feel pain. . . . No, my films are more about pleasure, sensuality, and living—about the celebration of living. Don't forget, you have to be conscious that for this celebration of absolute pleasure, often you have to pay a very high price. But the price is parallel with the pleasure. This is the theory of *Matador.* If you can find an absolute pleasure, you also have to pay an absolute price. And in the reference to *Duel in the Sun*, there is, of course, what you said, but what was more important for me in this scene is just that when the ex-matador and lawyer come to the cinema, they look at the screen and see their future. It's like when you look into a magic crystal ball. When you go to the cinema, the cinema reflects not your life but your end. And it was exactly the ending of *Duel in the Sun* that is the ending of *Matador*.

MK: But then both in *Matador* and *Law of Desire*, watching movies seems to be a very dangerous activity.

PA: No, the problem is that *your* mentality is far more rational than ours, than of the Spanish people. And perhaps all of these terrible things are here inside my films. But I don't see these elements so clearly. I'm unconscious of them. I don't want to be so conscious of all these things. You explain everything. I prefer just to inspire, to suggest, not to explain.

MK: I'm not really saying there are "terrible things" in your films, I'm just considering the implications of your choices—like the implications of having your last three films all end the same way, with an orgasmic climax in which two people are brought together in a passionate union that is somehow related to suicide and murder. In making this choice, aren't you romanticizing the price one has to pay for this absolute value? Isn't this a kind of romantic idealism that has connections with fascism since fascism also glamorizes death and sacrifice in the name of the idea?

PA: That sounds terrible! [laughs] . . . No, the moral of all my films is to get to a stage of greater freedom. *What Have I Done?* is about the liberation of women, even if it takes killing. It's very dangerous to see my films with conventional morality. I have my own morality. And so do my films. If you see *Matador* through a perspective of traditional morality, it's a dangerous film because it's just a celebration of killing. *Matador* is like a legend. I don't try to be realistic, it's very abstract, so you don't feel identification with the things that are happening, but with the sensibility of this kind of romanticism. I hope that there is not this kind of fascist element in the celebration of murder. You know, murder happens. I'm not as, what should I say, as "naughty" as Patricia Highsmith. The kind of murder that horrifies me is the kind that happens in her novels—among regular people, where you agree with that murder. This is really immoral.

MK: I think it's your tone that prevents the spectator from taking these murders seriously or from seeing them in terms of traditional morality. I know you've been widely quoted as saying you want to make films as if Franco had never existed, and I think that desire may be related to your refusal to see this potential connection between romantic love and fascism.

PA: Perhaps I didn't fully understand what you said before about my glorification of violence.

MK: It's not just violence, it's violence in the name of a noble sacrifice, which one can also find in Christianity. For example, Tina has an altar in which she puts the image of the Virgin next to that of Marilyn Monroe and Liz Taylor. . . .

PA: The Spanish people are known to be very religious. But it's not true. What we do in general is to adapt religion for our own needs, as Tina does. She needs to lean on something because she feels very much alone. Religion is there to make her feel better, to keep her company. And the altar contains, not only things of beauty, but all of her memories that accompany her, that prevent her from feeling so lonely. This is the kind of religion she needs. For her, there's a Virgin and a dictator, and even the toys of the young girl.

MK: Yes, but doesn't the altar serve as the backdrop for the final reunion between Pablo and Antonio, for their Passion?

PA: Yes, in the end they form part of the altar, they become religious figuros.

MK: That's precisely what I mean. You glorify their kind of romantic love by turning it into a religion, by mystifying it with the same ideological trappings that helped to glorify fascism. But with lots of humor. . . . Maybe it's time to turn to another crucial institution that was glorified by Franco, the family. In one interview you noted that Wim Wenders chose a melodrama about the family (*Paris, Texas*) to win the hearts of American spectators.

PA: That was just a joke. I like using the family very much.

MK: In Spanish films, the family is typically made up of cruel mothers, absent, mythified fathers, and stunted, precocious children. And there seems to be a special Spanish version of the Oedipal narrative with a series of displacements of desire and hostility between the mother and the father. Sometimes the object of desire for the son is transferred from mother to father as in *Law of Desire,* but mostly there's a displacement of the hostility, usually directed at the father, onto the mother. I don't find this dynamic in any other national cinema. And this is particularly odd since patriarchal power is so strong, or at least was so strong in Spain under Franco. Is it that the father is so threatening, the son has to displace his hostility onto the mother? Why do you think there's so much hostility directed toward the mother?

PA: I don't know. I defended the mother in *What Have I Done?* Of course, there was also a bad mother next door, but you actually find this kind of mother in Spain—the one who is so repressive to her children.

MK: Yes, but in *Matador* the only evil character is not the serial murderers, but Ángel's repressive mother from Opus Dei.

PA: Yes, I find this kind of mother very hateful, but there are several other mothers in that film. . . . I feel very close to the mother. The idea of motherhood is very important in Spain. The father was frequently absent in Spain. It's as if the mother represents the law, the police. It's very curious because in my next film project, I have two young girls kill their mother. When you kill the mother, you kill precisely everything you hate, all of those burdens that hang over you. In this film, I'm killing all of my education and all of the intolerance that is sick in Spain.

MK: Is this matricide an act of liberation, or is it suicidal?

PA: I don't want to psychoanalyze it. It's like killing the power. In my film, this is a very typical mother from the South, like Bernarda Alba. In order to frighten her two daughters, she tells them that the world is going to be destroyed and that they will be guilty. And the two girls run away. Then the two parents, both the father and the mother, supposedly die, but the mother doesn't really die. When the two girls become women, the mother suddenly appears like a ghost in order to drive them crazy, really crazy, because she behaves like a ghost. It's very surrealistic. At the end, the two girls have a duel with their mother and then, after they kill her, they discover that she was not a ghost, that she was alive. But she was very crazy. The mother's behavior is actually more murderous than that of the girls.

MK: It sounds fascinating. I can't think of any other national cinema that has so many matricides as the Spanish cinema. For example, in 1975, the year that Franco died, there were two major films in which matricide occurs—*Furtivos* (Poachers) and *Pascual Duarte*. And later in Saura's *Mamá Cumple Cien Años* (Mamá Turns 100), it's attempted again. And now your project! And, what's also strange, in Spanish films the killing of the father is only done by daughters, not by sons.

PA: It's true. . . . Fathers are not very present in my films. I don't know why they are not in my films. This is something I just feel. When I'm writing about relatives, I just put in mothers, but I try not to put in fathers. I avoid it. I don't know why. I guess I'm very Spanish.

MK: I guess you treat fathers like Franco, as if they never existed. . . . What is the name of your new project?

PA: I don't know whether I'm going to change it later, but now it's called *Distant Heels*. I remember when I was a child, it was a symbol of freedom for young girls to wear high heels, to smoke, and to wear trousers. And these two girls are wearing heels all the time. After running away, the two sisters live together, and the older remembers that she couldn't sleep until the moment that she heard the sound of distant heels coming from the corridor. I also like the title because it sounds like a western. All this happens in a desert in the South, and the look is like that.

MK: What qualities do you strive for in your mise-en-scène? Can you make any generalizations about that? The visual look seems quite different from film to film.

PA: Yes, they *are* different. I'm learning at the same time that I'm shooting. I didn't go to any film school. So everything I learned was learned while shooting. Also, I like so many different genres and want to go for very different qualities in each film. I have many different sides and want to develop them all. I'm not obsessed with style. I'd like each film to be absolutely different from the others in every possible way. This is a way of learning everything. And I don't want to get bored.

MK: What impact has your success in Berlin and New York with *Law of Desire* had on your new projects? Has it led to any concrete proposals for the future? Any international coproductions?

PA: For me the success merely means I can sell my films outside of Spain, and that's good for everybody. Right now I don't feel the temptation to make films outside of Spain because here I can work easier and faster and because it's the culture I know better than any other. I'm sure I'll make a film outside of Spain one day, but not now, not for the moment. Someday I would like to make a film in English, but later. Perhaps I'm lazy. But I want to keep working in this way. I want to feel very independent, and now I have to defend my independence even more than before.

Excerpt from Marsha Kinder, "Pleasure and the New Spanish Mentality: A Conversation with Pedro Almodóvar," *Film Quarterly* 41.1 (Fall 1987): 33–44.

This conversation took place on May 25, 1987, at Pedro Almodóvar's *piso* in Madrid. It was made possible by a research grant from the Comité Conjunto Hispano Norteamericano para la Cooperación Cultural y Educativa.

Pedro Almodóvar

Q: In *Law of Desire* [1987], the transsexual played by Carmen Maura goes into the church of the school where she studied as a boy. She finds a priest playing the organ in the choir. The priest asks her who she is. Carmen confesses to him that she had been a pupil at the school and that he [the priest] had been in love with him. Is that the origin of *Bad Education*?

A: More or less. Long before that, I had written a short story in which a transvestite goes back to the school where he had studied to blackmail the priests who had harassed him when he was a boy. While filming *Law of Desire* I remembered that story, and it gave me the idea of Carmen's character going into the church at his school and meeting a priest who loved him when she was a boy. By then I was considering the idea of developing the short story in detail. Carmen is a foreshadow of Zahara.

Q: There is also a film director in *Law of Desire*?

A: Yes, and like Fele Martínez's character he mixes his personal desires with his work, and in the end he pays a very high price for it. I've always been interested by the story of the artist who works with his own guts. It's a fascinating adventure even if it never ends well.

Q: In your first statements you denied that the film is autobiographical.

A: Paco Umbral says that everything that isn't autobiographical is plagiarism. The film is autobiographical, but in a deeper sense. I am behind those characters, but I'm not telling my life story.

Q: I believe you were the soloist in your school choir . . .

A: Yes. And I sang all the time, masses in Latin, motets, etc. I sang at all the religious ceremonies and the celebrations. And I guess I didn't do it badly. The priests recorded some of the songs I sang and played them at the door of the church to attract the faithful. And I remember that we filled the church. I'd give anything to recover those tapes, but I don't think they exist. What I most enjoyed in my time at school were the religious ceremonies. I'm agnostic, but I think the Catholic liturgy has a dazzling richness, it fascinates me and moves me. But it's been a long time since I went to mass. I don't know what it's like now.

Q: Does Fr. Manolo exist?

A: Yes, as a character.

Q: But did he really exist?

A: No. He's a made-up character, although for some scenes I was inspired by two priests at school.

Q: For what scenes in particular?

A: The harassment by the river and in the sacristy.

Q: Are they real scenes?

A: Two schoolmates told me about them. If you're a boarder at a school you eventually find out about everything.

Q: If the two people who were the inspiration for Fr. Manolo are alive, aren't you afraid they may react?

A: Admitting that they were being alluded to would be like accusing themselves. I'm a director and a scriptwriter. For me, Fr. Manolo is a character, one with whom, I should mention in passing, I'm very satisfied. The character isn't a weapon thrown against the Catholic church (which does have a lot of problems to solve, including its priests' sexuality. If celibacy didn't exist, there wouldn't be so many cases of abuse). I didn't create Fr. Manolo and his prolongation, Mr. Berenguer, in order to attack the church. They are elements that allow me to talk about two of the many faces of passion. When Fr. Manolo is played by Daniel Giménez-Cacho, the passion he feels for the boy and his abuse of power make him into an executioner. When he calls himself Mr. Berenguer and has cast off his habits and falls in love with Juan, the terrible character plays the opposite role in the roulette of passion. Now he is a victim. The film is inconceivable without those two characters, who are really one, and without their incarnation by Daniel Giménez-Cacho and Lluis Homar, respectively. Although they are two veterans, they were two great discoveries for me. I can never thank them enough for their lack of prejudice, their depth, and their unending willingness to satisfy all the demands of a director as insatiable as I am.

Q: What can you tell me about the rest of the cast?

A: They are superb. Fele Martínez, Francisco Boira, the kids, Javier Cámara, Albert Ferreiro, Petra Martínez, Francisco Maestre, and, naturally, Gael. It's a miracle to get it right with all the actors, especially when you don't know any of them, except Javier and Fele.

Q: Fele doesn't seem like himself, physically.

A: I made him slim down and train for four or five months, until he got another [better] body, another physical attitude. He was delighted, because everyone found him much sexier. As well as the physical aspect, we also worked on his tone of voice. I lowered its tessitura. He gave the character his heart, all of it, and his skin. I believe that from now on Fele will do other kinds of roles, less teen, more adult. He's an all-round actor. He can span the two extremes, torrid drama and crazy comedy. As happens in a different way with Javier Cámara.

Javier is very versatile. He works in all the media (cinema, television, theater, cabaret) and in all the genres. In *Talk to Her,* even though the role was dramatic, I discovered his gift for humour, and even though it's brief, his character in *Bad Education* was like an oasis for the whole crew. Javier is a comedian virtuoso. He has that special gift that goes beyond acting and that can't be learned. His composition of "Paca" is rich, exhaustive, human, hilarious, dangerous for whoever is at his side because you only have eyes for him. A natural "scene stealer."

Q: Poor Gael!

A: Not in the slightest. Gael is going to work a lot, and he's going to make lots of money.

Q: How and why did you choose him, after cross-dressing every Spanish actor in the prime of young manhood?

A: By auditioning him two or three times, like everyone else.

Q: What did he have that the others didn't?

A: He was very attractive as a boy and as a girl, and that was essential for understanding his character's relationship with the others, the intensity with which everyone became obsessed with him.

Q: Is Gael the villain of the story?

A: *Bad Education* is the opposite of a film with good guys and villains. In any case, I never judge characters whatever they do. My job is to "represent them," "explain them in all their complexity," and come up with an entertaining spectacle with all that. It isn't good for a film that the director judges his characters, even if they do atrocious things. Juan, the base-character that Gael plays, is a guy who doesn't stop at anything as long as he achieves his ambitions. He is capable of killing, if the situation comes up, of seducing and of having sex with men and women depending on his convenience. His absolute lack of scruples gives him an incredible strength and makes of him a walking menace. But if you don't cross his ambition's path, Juan is a normal guy who can live perfectly integrated in society without anyone detecting the danger that he brings along. I like to compare it to Patricia Highsmith's amoral characters, Ripley, for example, who is not affected morally by murders but ends up refining them, cultivating them, and making them more charming. Considering the movie as a dark "thriller," as I said before, the character of Gael represents the typical femme fatale (in his case, "enfant terrible") because he leads all the characters who come in contact with him to their downfall. And *Downfall (Perdición)* is the Spanish title for *Double Indemnity* (by the genius Billy Wilder), "noirest" among the "noir," to which I'm paying homage. Juan and Mr. Berenguer go to the Museum of Giant Figures in Valencia to plan a murder. Juan tells his lover that after they carry it out they mustn't see each other for a while. With the naïveté of the typical manipulated lover, Mr. Berenguer thought that the murder would unite them forever, but on the contrary, it drives them apart. And he can't bear that idea, but it's too late to avoid it.

This scene is a reference (and reverence) to the scene in the supermarket in *Double Indemnity*. Even though I really like how it turned out, I'm aware that no film in color can surpass the image of Barbara Stanwyck in a curly blonde wig and large dark glasses, surrounded by stacks of canned food, all of it, including Fred MacMurray, in glorious black and white.

Q: What was it like working with Gael?

A: A challenge, for him and for me. It isn't easy to play a character that is actually three, especially when two of them are very different physically. I guess it's the hardest work that Gael has done to date. On top of the difficulty of changing sex and not looking grotesque, there was the accent. I wanted him to speak Spanish, not Mexican, which is very different. . . .

Q: Are you satisfied with the result?

A: Yes. I hope that the spectators won't let themselves be influenced by the fact that one of his characters is so hateful. To end up, I don't want to forget Alberto Ferreiro, Francisco Maestre, Petra Martínez, and the kids. They were all wonderful surprises. With Raúl García and Ignacio Pérez [the kids], I hit the jackpot. You never know what can happen with one child, never mind two. I have no experience with child actors, and I think the result is very moving. I'm very proud of that part of the film (the story of the two boys and their relationship with God and Fr. Manolo), perhaps because before I started shooting it seemed to be the most difficult and most delicate part. I'm very grateful to Joserra Cadiñanos, the casting director, who during the shooting helped me explain to Ignacio and Raúl what they were doing and why they were doing it. Joserra was my best intermediary.

Q: The structure of *Bad Education* is at least as complicated as that of *Talk to Her*. . . .

A: I think it's even more so. As in *Talk to Her*, in *Bad Education* there is a film-within-a-film, but in this case it lasts half an hour, which is even more risky. Really, the film tells three stories, about three concentric triangles, which in the end turn out to be just one story.

Q: The story of a director-scriptwriter who is looking for a story. . . .

A: And who finds it. As Truman Capote said, quoting St. Teresa, "There are more tears shed over answered prayers than over unanswered prayers."

Q: Why so many voiceovers?

A: The voiceover is used to explain what isn't seen and to speed up the narration's rhythm. It is as if a character in the movie visits you, sits down in front of you at the table, and sums up part of his or her story. Voiceovers have been essential for me to shift from one story to the other, from one period to the other. The good thing about having the two protagonists, one a film director (that is to say, a narrator, someone who investigates so that everything is understood) and the other possessing a tight secretive attitude, an intrinsic quality of the imposter's nature, the good thing about having these two opposed characters, I say, is that it makes us understand lots of keys to Gael's character through the director [Fele Martínez]. The spectator knows what Fele knows, so he or she identifies with Fele, and it's his eyes and his "voiceovers" that explain his discoveries about himself and the mysterious and ferocious figure of Gael-Juan.

Brothers

Q: One of the elements in the plot that works best is when we discover that two of the characters are brothers.

A: Yes, and I'd like to keep that a secret. I adore the feeling of fraternity, and I've always liked films about siblings: Warren Beatty getting a beating in a parking lot for defending the honour of his sister, Barbara Loden, in *Splendor in the Grass*. Legs Diamond, in the film by Budd Boetticher, getting caught because of his brother's carelessness. The Bonnie and Clyde gang, led by two brothers. The entire *Godfather* saga has given us marvelous scenes of siblings who love each other, beat each other up, protect each other, and kill each other. All of Ma Barker's children in *No Orchids for Miss Blandish* [written by James Hadley Chase, directed by John L. Clowes]. *Bloody Mama,* by Roger Corman. Fierce mothers, leaders of gangs made up of their own children. I'm moved by all of Alain Delon's brothers in *Rocco and His Brothers.* Even Michael Jackson and Latoya Jackson, deformed mirrors of each other. Natalie Wood and George Chakiris in *West Side Story.* Hayley Mills playing her own twin in *The Parent Trap,* the Siamese twins in *Sisters,* by early Brian de Palma. The Marx brothers in any of their films. The touching Harry Dean Stanton in *Paris, Texas,* and his silent visit to his brother, Dean Stockwell. The two Mills sisters in *Fallen Angel,* by Preminger, the two delightful spinsters in *Arsenic and Old Lace,* and Shelley Winters's little orphans, pursued by the evil Robert Mitchum in *The Night of the Hunter.* And even, although Raymond Chandler's dialogue prevented the slightest sentimentality, Lauren Bacall defending her indefensible sister in *The Big Sleep.* At times the fraternal relationship gets complicated (how could it not!) when there is sex. I love Sam Shepard's play *Fool for Love,* and the wonderful novel *Middlesex* in which a brother and sister even get married. Fraternity is a sentiment in disuse, replaced in present-day life by friendship, but it isn't exactly the same; fraternity springs from two great sentiments, love and friendship, united by something as unfathomable as consanguinity.

Among the films about siblings that I remember, I haven't mentioned *Whatever Happened to Baby Jane?* (Robert Aldrich), a "grand guignol" in which the two immense leading ladies are elevated in category and genre. Two sisters, both of them former child stars, live together when they are adults, even though they hate each other. One of them (Bette Davis) ends up killing the other (Joan Crawford).

There is something of this in *Bad Education,* although in a hidden way. When they were little, Juan (Ángel Andrade) was jealous of his older brother Ignacio because he was better at everything. Jealousy in younger siblings is very common. But in Juan's case, it grew over the years. The two boys wanted to be "artistes." Everything was easy for Ignacio: singing, dancing, writing, reciting, transforming himself, and acting. Everything that Juan would have liked to do, Ignacio did better. And Juan hated him in silence until Ignacio gave him cause to hate him openly when he began to take drugs and dress as a woman in the little town where they lived. Family life was absolute hell because of Ignacio. The mother, who had a weak heart, was in an unbearable situation. The father couldn't stand the shame and started to drink more and more, until one winter's day they found him dead in the street, in a frozen puddle. Out of obedience to his mother, and in his own interest, Juan went to live with his brother in Valencia. He enrolled in an acting school and kept an eye on Ignacio, so that his mother wouldn't worry so much. It was the start of democracy in Spain, and in Valencia Ignacio lived a very free life, devoted to writing, to changing his body into that of a real woman, and to using heroin to anaesthetize the tension produced by his lifestyle.

Then Mr. Berenguer, Ignacio's old literature teacher, turned up. He had hung up his habits and was living in Valencia and working in a publishing house. The appearance of the former Fr. Manolo dynamites the two brothers' existence.

Q: After thirteen years, [*Tie Me Up! Tie Me Down!*], you're working with José Luis Alcaine again as director of photography.

A: What a great idea it was to call him! José Luis has done a splendid job. I barely had to tell him what I wanted. Music and photography are two abstract elements, hard to explain. I turn up for the shoot, laden with references, but the director of photography has to sense, guess, smell the atmosphere that goes best with the story. Or atmospheres, because in *Bad Education* there are a lot of films together, and very different aesthetics coexist within the same story. Alcaine was immensely inspired every day of this very hot shoot. As a professional he's at his peak, and I think we've both matured as people, and the result has been a perfect marriage.

Q: And [Jean-Paul] Gaultier?

A: I called him to dress Zahara, in particular her outfit for the show, which is a masterpiece in terms of cut and conception. It's a flesh-colored dress, tight-fitted to the neck like a second skin, that gives the impression of total nudity. The ass, the tits, and the pubis are made with sequins and brown and pink glass bead and tones. The dress in itself represents false, naked femininity. He also undertook to give a touch to the adult Ignacio's gabardines and shorts. Jean-Paul is like a big child. That's why he'll never make a vulgar dress. Working with him is great fun. I adore him.

Q: This is the fifth time you've worked with Alberto Iglesias. . . .

A: Alberto Iglesias is the only marvelous artist I know without any ego problems, the only one I make repeat the themes over and over again without his losing either his enthusiasm or his creativity. He is a musician and a person out of the ordinary. For this occasion, he has built a powerful, original column of sound on which the film rests, like a baby rests in its mother's arms. Alberto surprises me in every movie. After the mixing I cannot think of a musical costume that better suits *Bad Education* than the one that Alberto has created for it.

Q: To judge from the answers to your own questions, you give the impression of being very happy with this film.

A: I'm never happy, but, well . . . let's say I'm pretty cheerful.

Q: Future projects?

A: To recover my sleep and my waistline.

Pepi, Luci, Bom, y otras chicas del montón (Pepi, Luci, Bom, and Other Girls
on the Heap; 1980)
Production Company: Figaro Films
Producer: Pepón Corominas
Script: Pedro Almodóvar
Executive Producer: Félix Rotaeta
Director of Photography: Paco Femenia
Editor: José Salcedo
Running time: 80 minutes
Cast: Carmen Maura (Pepi), Félix Rotaeta (policeman), Alaska [Olvido
Gara] (Bom), Eva Siva (Luci), Kiti Manver (flamenco rock artiste), Julieta
Serrano (actress), Fabio de Miguel [McNamara] (Roxy)

Laberinto de pasiones (Labyrinth of Passions; 1982)
Production Company: Alphaville
Script: Pedro Almodóvar
Production Manager: Andrés Santana
Director of Photography: Ángel Luis Fernández
Editor: José Salcedo
Running time: 100 minutes
Cast: Cecilia Roth (Sexilia), Imanol Arias (Riza), Marta Fernández Muro
(Queti), Fernando Vivanco (doctor), Helga Liné (Toraya), Ofelia Angélica
(Susana), Antonio Banderas (Sadec), Luis Ciges (dry cleaner)

Entre tinieblas (Dark Habits; 1983)
Production Company: Tesauro
Script: Pedro Almodóvar
Production Manager: Luis Calvo
Director of Photography: Ángel Luis Fernández
Editor: José Salcedo
Costume: Teresa Nieto Morán, Francis Montesinos

Running time: 115 minutes
Cast: Cristina Pascual (Yolanda), Julieta Serrano (Mother Superior), Marisa
   Paredes (Sister Manure), Chus Lampreave (Sister Rat), Carmen Maura
   (Sister Damned), Lina Canalejas (Sister Snake), Mary Carrillo (Marquesa)

¿Qué he hecho yo para merecer esto? (What Have I Done to Deserve This?;
   1984)
Production Company: Tesauro
Script: Pedro Almodóvar
Production Manager: Luis Briales
Director of Photography: Ángel Luis Fernández
Music: Bernardo Bonezzi
Editor: José Salcedo
Costume: Cecilia Roth
Running time: 102 minutes
Cast: Carmen Maura (Gloria), Ángel de Andrés López (Antonio), Chus
   Lampreave (grandmother), Verónica Forqué (Cristal), Kiti Manver (Juani),
   Juan Martínez (Toni), Miguel Ángel Herranz (Miguel), Katia Loritz (Ingrid
   Müller), Gonzalo Suárez (Lucas), Emilio Gutiérrez Caba (Pedro), Amparo
   Soler Leal (Patricia)

Matador (1986)
Production Company: Iberoamericana (and TVE)
Script: Pedro Almodóvar and Jesús Ferrero
Executive Producer: Andrés Vicente Gómez
Director of Photography: Ángel Luis Fernández
Music: Bernardo Bonezzi
Editor: José Salcedo
Costume: José María Cossío
Running time: 96 minutes
Cast: Assumpta Serna (María), Nacho Martínez (Diego), Antonio Banderas
   (Ángel), Eva Cobo (Eva), Julieta Serrano (Berta), Chus Lampreave (Pilar),
   Carmen Maura (Julia), Eusebio Pencela (inspector)

La ley del deseo (Law of Desire; 1987)
Production Company: El Deseo S.A.
Script: Pedro Almodóvar
Executive Producer: Miguel A. Pérez Campos
Production Manager: Esther García
Director of Photography: Ángel Luis Fernández
Editor: José Salcedo
Costume: José María Cossío
Running time: 100 minutes

Cast: Eusebio Poncela (Pablo), Carmen Maura (Tina), Antonio Banderas (Antonio), Miguel Molina (Juan), Manuela Velasco (Ada), Bibi Andersen (Ada's mother), Fernando Guillén (inspector), Fernando G. Cuervo (detective), Nacho Martínez (doctor), Helga Liné (Antonio's mother)

Mujeres al borde de un ataque de nervios (Women on the Verge of a Nervous Breakdown; 1988)
Production Company: El Deseo S.A.
Script: Pedro Almodóvar
Executive Producer: Agustín Almodóvar
Production Manager: Esther García
Director of Photography: José Luis Alcaine
Editor: José Salcedo
Music: Bernardo Bonezzi
Costume: José María Cossío
Running time: 105 minutes
Cast: Carmen Maura (Pepa), Fernando Guillén (Iván), Julieta Serrano (Lucía), Antonio Banderas (Carlos), Rossy de Palma (Marisa), María Barranco (Candela), Kiti Manver (Paulina), Chus Lampreave (doorwoman), Loles León (receptionist), Willy Montesinos (taxi driver)

¡Atame! (Tie Me Up! Tie Me Down!; 1989)
Production Company: El Deseo S.A.
Script: Pedro Almodóvar
Executive Producer: Agustín Almodóvar
Production Manager: Esther García
Director of Photography: José Louis Alcaine
Editor: José Salcedo
Music: Ennio Morricone
Costume: José María Cossío
Running time: 101 minutes
Cast: Victoria Abril (Marina), Antonio Banderas (Ricky), Loles León (Lola), Julieta Serrano (Alma), María Barranco (doctor), Rossy de Palma (drug dealer), Francisco Rabal (Máximo Espejo)

Tacones lejanos (High Heels; 1991)
Production Company: El Deseo S.A., Ciby 2000
Script: Pedro Almodóvar
Executive Producer: Agustín Almodóvar
Production Manager: Esther García
Director of Photography: Alfredo Mayo
Editor: José Salcedo
Music: Ryuichi Sakamoto

Costume: José María Cossío, Giorgio Armani, Chanel
Running time: 113 minutes
Cast: Victoria Abril (Rebecca), Marisa Paredes (Becky), Miguel Bosé
(Femme Letal/Judge Domínguez), Feodor Atkine (Manuel), Pedro Díez
del Corral (Alberto), Ana Lizarán (Margarita), Míriam Díaz Aroca (Isabel),
Mayrata O'Wisiedo (Judge's mother)

Kika (1993)
Production Company: El Deseo S.A., Ciby 2000
Script: Pedro Almodóvar
Executive Producer: Agustín Almodóvar
Production Manager: Esther García
Director of Photography: Alfredo Mayo
Editor: José Salcedo
Costume: Jean-Paul Gaultier, Gianni Versace, José María Cossío
Running time: 112 minutes
Cast: Verónica Forqué (Kika), Peter Coyote (Nick), Victoria Abril (Andrea),
Alex Casanovas (Ramón), Rossy de Palma (Juana), Santiago Lajusticia
(Paul Bazzo), Anabel Alonso (Amparo), Bibi Andersen (Susana), Charo
López (Ramón's mother)

La flor de mi secreto (The Flower of My Secret; 1995)
Production Manager: Esther García
Production Company: El Deseo S.A., Ciby 2000
Director of Photography: Affonso Beato
Editor: José Salcedo
Music: Alberto Iglesias
Costume: Hugo Mezcua
Running time: 90 minutes
Cast: Marisa Paredes (Leo), Juan Echanove (Ángel), Carmen Elías (Betty),
Rossy de Palma (Rosa), Chus Lampreave (Leo's mother), Kiti Manver
(Manuela), Joaquín Cortés (Antonio), Manuela Vargas (Blanca), Imanol
Arias (Paco)

Carne trémula (Live Flesh; 1997)
Production Company: El Deseo S.A., Ciby 2000, France 3
Script: Pedro Almodóvar (with Ray Loriga and Jorge Guerricaechevarría)
Executive Producer: Agustín Almodóvar
Production Manager: Esther García
Director of Photography: Affonso Beato
Editor: José Salcedo
Music: Alberto Iglesias
Costume: José María de Cossío

Running time: 103 minutes
Cast: Francesca Neri (Elena), Liberto Rabal (Víctor), Javier Bardem (David), Angela Molina (Clara), Pepe Sancho (Sancho), Pilar Bardem (Doña Centro), Penélope Cruz (Isabel)

Todo sobre mi madre (All about My Mother; 1999)
Production Company: El Deseo S.A., Renn Productions, France 2 Cinéma
Script: Pedro Almodóvar
Executive Producer: Agustín Almodóvar
Production Manager: Esther García
Director of Photography: Affonso Beato
Editor: José Salcedo
Music: Alberto Iglesías
Costume: José María Cossío
Running time: 101 minutes
Cast: Cecilia Roth (Manuela), Marisa Paredes (Huma Rojo), Candela Peña (Nina), Antonia San Juan (La Agrado), Penélope Cruz (Hermana Rosa), Rosa María Sardá (Rosa's mother), Fernando Fernán Gómez (Rosa's father), Fernando Guillén (doctor), Toni Cantó (Lola), Eloy Azorín (Estéban), Carlos Lozano (Mario), Lluís Pasqual (himself)

Hable con ella (Talk to Her; 2002)
Production Company: El Deseo S.A.
Script: Pedro Almodóvar
Producer: Agustín Almodóvar
Head of Production: Esther García
Director of Photography: Javier Aguirresarobe
Editor: José Salcedo
Music: Alberto Iglesias
Costume: Sonia Grande
Running time: 112 minutes
Cast: Darío Grandinetti (Marco), Javier Cámara (Benigno), Rosario Flores (Lydia), Leonor Watling (Alicia), Geraldine Chaplin (Katerina).

La mala educación (Bad Education; 2004)
Production Company: El Deseo S.A.
Script: Pedro Almodóvar
Producer: Agustín Almodóvar
Executive Producer: Esther García
Director of Photography: José Luis Alcaine AEC
Editor: José Salcedo
Music: Alberto Iglesias
Art Director: Antxon Gómez
Sound: Micuel Rejas

Costumes: Paco Delgado, with special collaboration of Jean-Paul Gaultier
Running time: 122 minutes
Cast: Gael García Bernal (Ángel/Juan/Zahara), Fele Martínez (Enrique
  Goded), Javier Cámara (Paquito), Daniel Giménez-Cacho (Father
  Manolo), Lluis Homar (Mr. Berenguer), Francisco Boira (Ignacio),
  Francisco Maestre (Father José), Juan Fernández (Martín), Ignacio Pérez
  (Ignacio kid), Raúl García Forneiro (Enrique kid), Alberto Ferreiro
  (Enrique Serrano), Petra Martínez (Ignacio's mother), Sandra Nancy
  (Doll), Roberto Hoyas (Galicia's barman)

Bibliography |

Alabadejo, Miguel, Mario Arias, and José A. Hergueta. *Los fantasmas del deseo: A propósito de Pedro Almodóvar.* Madrid: Aula 7, 1988.

Allinson, Mark. *A Spanish Labyrinth: The Films of Pedro Almodóvar.* London and New York: I. B. Tauris, 2001.

———. "The Construction of Youth in Spain in the 1980s and 1990s." In *Contemporary Spanish Cultural Studies.* Ed. Barry Jordan and Rikki Morgan-Tamosunas. London: Arnold, 2000. 265–73.

———. *Un laberinto español: Las películas de Pedro Almodóvar.* Madrid: Semana de Cine Experimental de Madrid y 8 1/2, 2003.

Almodóvar, Pedro. *¡Atame!* Press-book, 1989.

———. *La flor de mi secreto.* Barcelona: Plaza y Janés, 1995.

———. *La flor de mi secreto.* Press-book, 1995.

———. "Génesis de Kika." *El País,* November 5, 1993, 11.

———. *Hable con ella.* Press-book, 2002.

———. "Industria e hipocresía," *El País,* April 22, 1990, 11.

——— *La mala educación: Guión cinematográfico de Pedro Almodóvar.* Madrid: Ocho y Medio Libros de Cine y El Deseo S.A., 2004.

———. *La mala educación.* Press-book, 2004.

———. *Patty Diphusa y otros textos.* Rev. ed. Barcelona: Editorial Anagrama, 1998.

———. *Tacones lejanos.* Press-book, 1991.

———. *Todo sobre mi madre.* Press-book, 2000.

Alvarez, Rosa, and Belén Frías. *Vicente Aranda: El cine como pasión.* Valladolid: 36 Semana Internacional deCine, 1991.

Boquerini (Francisco Blanco). *Pedro Almodóvar.* Madrid: JC, 1989.

Boyero, Carlos. "La moda Almodóvar." *Casablanca* 23 (November 1982): 43–45.

Certeau, Michel de. *The Practice of Everyday Life.* Trans. Steven Rendell. Berkeley: University of California Press, 1984.

Colmeiro, José. "Del rosa al negro: Subtextos culturales en *La flor de mi secreto.*" *Arizona Journal of Hispanic Cultural Studies* 1 (1997): 115–28.

Colmenero Salgado, Silvia. *Pedro Almodóvar: Todo sobre mi madre*. Barcelona: Ediciones Paidós, 2001.

Corliss, Richard. "Live Flesh." *Time*, February 23, 1998, 90.

Corrigan, Timothy. *A Cinema without Walls: Movies and Culture after Vietnam*. New Brunswick, N.J.: Rutgers University Press, 1991.

D'Lugo, Marvin. "Almodóvar's City of Desire." In *Post-Franco, Postmodern: The Films of Pedro Almodóvar*. Ed. Kathleen M. Vernon and Barbara Morris. Westport Conn.: Greenwood Press, 1995. 125–44.

Deleyto, Celestino. "Postmodernism and Parody in Almodóvar's *Mujeres al borde de un ataque de nervios*." *Forum for Modern Language Studies* 31.1 (1995): 49–63.

Edwards, Gwynne. *Almodóvar: Labyrinths of Passion*. London: Peter Owen, 2001.

Elsaesser, Thomas. "Tales of Sound and Fury: Observations on the Family Melodrama." In *Home Is Where the Heart Is: Studies in Melodrama and the Woman's Film*. Ed. Christine Gledhill. London: BFI Publishing, 1987. 43–69.

Escudero, Javier. "Rosa Montero y Pedro Almodóvar: Miseria y estilización de *la movida madrileña*." *Arizona Journal of Hispanic Cultural Studies* 2 (1998): 147–61.

Evans, Peter W. "Almodóvar's *Matador*: Genre, Subjectivity, and Desire." *Bulletin of Hispanic Studies* 70.3 (July, 1993): 325–35.

———. *Women on the Verge of a Nervous Breakdown*. London: BFI Publishing, 1996.

Fuentes, Víctor. "Almodóvar's Postmodern Cinema: A Work in Progress." In *Post-Franco, Postmodern: The Films of Pedro Almodóvar*. Ed. Kathleen M. Vernon and Barbarba Morris. Westport, Conn.: Greenwood Press, 1995. 155–70.

Galán, Diego. "Con Goucho Marx y Mae West." *El País*, October 30, 1980.

Gallero, J. L. *Sólo se vive una vez: Esplendor y ruina de la movida madrileña*. Madrid: Ardora Editores, 1991.

García Canclini, Néstor. *Culturas híbridas: Estrategias para entrar y salir de la modernidad*. México: Editorial Grijalbo, 1989.

García de León, María Antonia, and Teresa Maldonado. *Pedro Almodóvar, la otra España cañí (sociología y crítica cinematográficas)*. Ciudad Real: Area de Cultura, 1989.

Gómez, Andrés Vicente. *El sueño loco de Andrés Vicente Gómez*. Málaga: Festival de cine español de Mála, 2001.

Graham, Helen. "Popular Culture in the 'Years of Hunger.'" In *Spanish Cultural Studies, an Introduction: The Struggle for Modernity*. Ed. Helen Graham and Jo Labanyi. New York: Oxford University Press, 1995. 237–45.

Graham, Helen, and Jo Labanyi, eds. *Spanish Cultural Studies, an Introduction: The Struggle for Modernity*. New York: Oxford University Press, 1995.

Gubern, Román. "Universal gracias a su fuerza local." *El Mundo*, March 28, 2000.

Hall, Stuart. "European Cinema on the Verge of a Nervous Breakdown." In *Screening Europe: Image and Identity in Contemporary European Cinema*. Ed. Duncan Petrie. London: BFI Working Papers, 1992. 45–53.

Harguindey, Ángel S. "Grab the Fame and Run." In *Pedro Almodóvar Interviews*. Ed. Paula Willoquet-Maricondi. Jackson: University of Mississippi Press, 2004. 32–39.

Hirschberg, Lynn. "The Redeemer." *New York Times Magazine*, September 5, 2004, 24–27, 38–45, 70.

Holguín, Antonio. *Pedro Almodóvar*. Madrid: Ediciones Cátedra, 1994.

Jameson, Fredric. *Postmodernism; or, The Cultural Logic of Late Capitalism*. Durham, N.C.: Duke University Press, 1991.

Kael, Pauline. "Red on Red." In *Hooked*. New York: E. P. Dutton, 1989. 466–69.

Kinder, Marsha. *Blood Cinema: The Reconstruction of National Identity in Spain*. Berkeley: University of California Press, 1993.

———. "From Matricide to Mother Love in Almodóvar's *High Heels*." In *Post-Franco, Postmodern: The Films of Pedro Almodóvar*. Ed. Kathleen M. Vernon and Barbara Morris. Westport, Conn.: Greenwood Press, 1995. 145–53.

———. "Pleasure and the New Spanish Mentality: A Conversation with Pedro Almodóvar." *Film Quarterly* 41.1 (Fall 1987): 33–44.

———. "Refiguring Socialist Spain: An Introduction." In *Refiguring Spain: Cinema/Media/Representation*. Ed. Marsha Kinder. Durham, N.C.: Duke University Press, 1997. 1–32.

———. "Reinventing the Motherland: Almodóvar's Brain-Dead Trilogy." *Journal of Spanish Cultural Studies* 6.3 (October 2004): 245–60.

LaPlace, Maria. "Producing and Consuming the Woman's Film: Discursive Struggle in *Now Voyager*." In *Home Is Where the Heart Is: Studies in Melodrama and the Woman's Film*. Ed. Christine Gledhill. London: BFI Publishing, 1987. 138–66.

Leavitt, David. "Almodóvar on the Verge." *New York Times Magazine*, April 22, 1990, 36–42.

Lev, Leora. "Tauromachy as a Spectacle of Gender Revision." In *Post-Franco, Postmodern: The Films of Pedro Almodóvar*. Ed. Kathleen M. Vernon and Barbara Morris. Westport, Conn.: Greenwood Press, 1995. 73–86.

Llauradó, Anna. "Entrevista con Pedro Almodóvar." *Dirigido por* 108 (October 1983): 10–13.

López, Betty. "Pedro Almodóvar: Todos los hermanos eran homosexuales." *Fotogramas* 1723 (October 1986): 51–53.

Mackenzie, Suzi. "All about My Father." In *Pedro Almodóvar Interviews*. Ed. Paula Willoquet-Maricondi. Jackson: University of Mississippi Press, 2004. 154–61.

Mandrell, James. "Sense and Sensibility, or Latent Heterosexuality and *Laberinto de pasiones*." In *Post-Franco, Postmodern: The Films of Pedro Almodóvar*.

Ed. Kathleen M. Vernon and Barbara Morris. Westport, Conn: Greenwood Press, 1995. 41–57.

Marsh, Steven. "Masculinity, Monuments, and Movement: Gender and the City of Madrid in Pedro Almodóvar's *Carne trémula* (1997)." In *Gender and Spanish Cinema*. Ed. Steven Marsh and Parvarti Nair. Oxford: Berg, 2004. 53–70.

Martin-Márquez, Susan. *Feminist Discourse and Spanish Cinema*. Oxford: Oxford University Press, 1999.

Mazierska, Ewa, and Laura Rascaroli. *From Moscow to Madrid: Postmodern Cities, European Cinema*. London: I. B. Tauris, 2003.

Mira, Alberto. *De Sodoma a Chueca: Una historia cultural de la homosexualidad en España en el siglo XX*. Barcelona: Editorial Egales, 2004.

———. "Laws of Silence: Homosexual Identity and Visibility in Contemporary Spanish Culture." In *Contemporary Spanish Cultural Studies*. Ed. Barry Jordan and Rikki Morgan-Tamosunas. London: Arnold, 2000. 241–50.

Mitchell, Elvis. "A Time When Loyalty Overrides Love." *New York Times*, October 12, 2002, B9.

Montano, Alicia G. "Almodóvar vuelve al cole." *Fotogramas* 1925 (March 2004): 112–19.

Nandorfy, Martha J. "*Tie Me Up! Tie Me Down!* Subverting the Glazed Gaze of American Melodrama and Film Theory." *Cineaction* 31 (1993): 50–61.

Noh, David. "Almodóvar's Secret." In *Pedro Almodóvar Interviews*. Ed. Paula Willoquet-Maricondo. Jackson: University of Mississippi Press, 2004. 119–25.

Pally, Marcia. "Pedro Almodóvar and the Camp Esthetic." *Cineaste* 18.1 (1990): 32–39.

Perriam, Chris. *Stars and Masculinities in Spanish Cinema*. Oxford: Oxford University Press, 2003.

Riambau, Estève. *Pepón Coromina, un productor con carisma*. Madrid: Academia de las Artes y Ciencias Cinematográficas de España, 1999.

Rioyo, Javier. "Todo sobre mi escuela." *El Periódico Dominical* 78 (March 14, 2004): 28–41.

Riquer i Permanyer, Borja de. "Social and Economic Change in a Time of Politicial Immobilism." In *Spanish Cultural Studies, an Introduction: The Struggle for Modernity*. Ed. Helen Graham and Jo Labanyi. New York: Oxford University Press, 1995. 259–71.

Sánchez-Biosca, Vicente. "El elixir aromático de la postmodernidad o la comedia según Pedro Almodóvar." In *Escritos sobre el cine español 1973–1987*. Ed. José A. Hurtado and Francisco M. Picó. Valencia: Ediciones Textos Filmoteca, 1995. 111–23.

Schaefer, Claudia. *Bored to Distraction: Cinema of Excess in End-of-the-Century Mexico and Spain*. Albany: State University of New York Press, 2003.

Smith, Paul Julian. *Desire Unlimited: The Cinema of Pedro Almodóvar.* 2d ed. London: Verso, 2000.

———. *Laws of Desire: Questions of Homosexuality in Spanish Writing and Film, 1960–1990.* Oxford: Clarendon Press, 1992.

———. *Vision Machines: Cinema, Literature, and Sexuality in Spain and Cuba, 1983–1993.* London: Verso, 1996.

Strauss, Frédéric. *Conversaciones con Pedro Almodóvar.* Verona: Ediciones Akal, 2001.

———. *Pedro Almodóvar: Entretien.* Paris: Cahiers du Cinéma, 2004.

———. *Pedro Almodóvar: Un cine visceral.* Madrid: El País/Aguilar, 1995.

Thompson, David. "*Tacones Lejanos* (High Heels)." *Sight and Sound* 1.12 (April 1992): 61–62.

Torres, Maruja. "Pedro Almodóvar: Life is a Bolero." In *Pedro Almodóvar Interviews.* Ed. Paula Willoquet-Maricondi. Jackson: University of Mississippi Press, 2004. 9–16.

Triana-Toribio, Núria. "Almodóvar's Melodramatic *Mise-en-scène:* Madrid as a Setting for Melodrama." *Bulletin of Hispanic Studies* 73.2 (April 1996): 179–89.

———. "A Punk Called Pedro: La Movida in the Films of Pedro Almodóvar." In *Contemporary Spanish Cultural Studies.* Ed. Barry Jordan and Rikki Morgan-Tamosunas. London: Arnold Press, 2000. 274–82.

———. "¿Qué he hecho yo para merecer esto?" In *Spanish Cinema: The Auteurist Tradition.* Ed. Peter William Evans. Oxford: Oxford University Press, 1999. 226–41.

———. *Spanish National Cinema.* London: Routledge, 2003.

Troyano, Ela. "Interview with Pedro Almodóvar: *Kika.*" In *Pedro Almodóvar Interviews* Ed. Paula Willoquet-Maricondo. Jackson: University of Mississippi Press, 2004. 102–9.

Valis, Noël. *Cursilería: Bad Taste, Kitsch, and Class in Modern Spain.* Durham, N.C.: Duke University Press, 2002.

Verdú, Vicente. "Españoles sin complejo." *El País semanal,* December 11, 1988, 38–45.

Vernon, Kathleen M. "Melodrama against Itself: Pedro Almodóvar's *What Have I Done to Deserve This?*" In *Post-Franco, Postmodern: The Films of Pedro Almodóvar.* Ed. Kathleen M. Vernon and Barbara Morris. Westport, Conn: Greenwood Press, 1995. 59–72.

———. "Scripting a Social Imaginary in/and Spanish Cinema." *Modes of Representation in Spanish Cinema* Ed. Jenaro Talens and Santos Zunzunegui. Minneapolis: University of Minnesota Press, 1998. 319–29.

Vernon, Kathleen M., and Barbara Morris, eds. *Post-Franco, Postmodern: The Films of Pedro Almodóvar.* Westport, Conn.: Greenwood Press, 1995.

Vidal, Nuria. *El cine de Pedro Almodóvar.* Barcelona: Destinolibro, 1988.

————. "No me gusta el mundo que me rodea." *El observador,* July 13, 1993, 45.

Vilarós, Teresa. *El mono del desencanto: Una crítica cultural de la transición española (1973–1993).* Madrid: Siglo Veintiuno Editores, 1998.

Williams, Linda. "Melancholy and Melodrama: Almodóvarian Grief and Lost Homosexual Attachments." *Journal of Spanish Cultural Studies* 5.3 (October 2004): 273–86.

Willoquet-Maricondi, Paula, ed. *Pedro Almodóvar Interviews.* Jackson: University of Mississippi Press, 2004.

Wilson, Andrew. *Beautiful Shadow: A Life of Patricia Highsmith.* New York: Bloomsbury, 2003.

Yarza, Alejandro. *Un caníbal en Madrid: La sensibilidad camp y el reciclaje de la historia en el cine de Pedro Almodóvar.* Madrid: Ediciones Libertarias, 1999.

Zunzunegui, Santos. *Historias de España: De qué hablamos cuando hablamos del cine español.* Valencia: Ediciones de la Filmoteca, 2002.

64; storytelling strategies, 2, 9, 10–11, 38; Super 8 movies of, 2, 15–16, 25; theatrical performances of, 8; threats from right, 128; thrillers of, 45–59; urban settings of, 74; use of comedy, 9, 26, 28, 61, 62, 133, 135–36; use of folkloric tradition, 5, 68; use of genres, 132–33; use of historical narrative, 97, 115, 120, 121; use of melodrama, 5, 6, 30–32, 38, 134–35; use of punk culture, 17–18; use of religious imagery, 5, 32, 58, 72–74; use of Spanish history, 116; Warhol's influence on, 7–8; in *What Have I Done to Deserve This?*, 42–43; Wilder's influence on, 134, 148; work with actors, 132; youth in Madrid, 14–15. *See also* Individual works

Al Qaeda, 128
Amante menguante (silent movie), 106
Amantes (Aranda), 82
Anachronism, in Spanish culture, 3
Andersen, Bibi, 103
Andrade, Angel, 151
Andrés-Lopez, Ángel de, 40; in *Women on the Verge of a Nervous Breakdown*, 60
Androgyny, in *Matador*, 49
Angélica, Ofelia, 27
Antonioni, Michelangelo, 13; *Blow-Up*, 83
Arabian Nights, in *Bad Education*, 122
Aranda, Vicente: *Amantes*, 82
Argentina, Dirty War in, 100
Arias, Imanol: in *The Flower of My Secret*, 86; in *Labyrinth of Passions*, 27
Arsenic and Old Lace, 150
Atkine, Feodor, 76
Atocha bombing (Madrid, 2004), 128
Autobiography: in Almodóvar's films, 7; in *Bad Education*, 11, 115, 129; in *The Flower of My Secret*, 85; in *Law of Desire*, 54, 55
Autumn Sonata (Bergman), 77
Aznar, José María, 128
Azorín, Eloy, 100

Bacall, Lauren, 151
Bad Education (Almodóvar), 59, 115–29;

Almodóvar directing, 127; Almodóvar on, 145–52; *Arabian Nights* in, 122; autobiography in, 11, 115, 129; brothers in, 150–52; cinematic quotes in, 116, 126; cultural history in, 120; debut of, 115, 128; differing aesthetics of, 152; family in, 151; femme fatale in, 124; film-within-a-film of, 149; Francoism in, 116, 121–22, 127; freeze-framing in, 120, 121; gay characters of, 6; historical narrative of, 97, 115, 120, 121, 123, 126–29; identity construction in, 122; Madrid in, 123; male characters of, 46; memory in, 123; music in, 125, 152; nostalgia in, 115–16; *pasotismo* of, 115; plot of, 110, 116, 118, 122; post-Franco Spain in, 122, 123; preface to script, 120; press book of, 3; protagonists of, 115; "self-interview" for, 126, 148–52; source of, 106, 123; Spanish release of, 128; story-within-a-story of, 123; structure of, 149; victimhood in, 121; "visitas" in, 118, 119–20, 121, 126; visual-narrative strategy of, 116, 119, 120–21, 122; voiceovers in, 149–50

Banderas, Antonio: film debut of, 28; and *High Heels*, 76, 79; in *Labyrinth of Passions*, 27, 28; in *Law of Desire*, 52, 54; in *Matador*, 47, 51, 52; in *Tie Me Up! Tie Me Down!*, 67, 69, 74, 75; in *Women on the Verge of a Nervous Breakdown*, 60, 62

Barcelona: in *All about My Mother*, 99, 100; film culture of, 15
Bardem, Javier, 93, 95
Bardem, Juan Antonio, 38; *Calle Mayor*, 12
Bardem, Pilar, 96, 98
Barranco, María, 62
Bass, Saul, 120
Bausch, Pina. *See* Pina Bausch dance company
Baxter, Ann, 102
Beatty, Warren, 37, 150
Beltrán, Lola, 65
Bennet, Joan, 125
Bergman, Ingmar: *Autumn Sonata*, 77
Bergman, Ingrid, 92

High Heels (Almodóvar), 75–80; commercial response to, 79–80; drag queens in, 78–79; family genealogy in, 78; historical images in, 78; human voice in, 77; Madrid in, 68; melodrama in, 77, 80; mother and daughter in, 77, 79; music in, 77, 125; narrative of, 76; patriarchy in, 79; personal identity in, 83; plot of, 76–77; production of, 68; self-referentiality in, 64

Highsmith, Patricia, 51, 140; *The Talented Mister Ripley,* 106, 124, 148; *This Sweet Sickness,* 106, 113

Hitchcock, Alfred: influence on Almodóvar, 51, 84, 120; *Psycho,* 42, 70; *Rear Window,* 84

Hoffman, Dustin, 56

Homar, Lluís, 119, 147

Homosexuality: in Almodóvar's films, 5–6; laws against, 14. *See also* Gay culture

Hostelot, Luis, 42

How to Marry a Millionaire, 62

Iberoamerican Films, 45

Identity: in *Labyrinth of Passions,* 28–29; performance of, 24–25; in *Tie Me Up! Tie Me Down!,* 69, 70, 83, 104. *See also* Gender identity; Sexual identity

Identity generation: in *All about My Mother,* 104, 105; in *Bad Education,* 122; through movies, 70, 83

Iglesia, Alex de, 98

Iglesias, Alberto, 113, 152

Imagery: historical, 78; juxtaposition with sound, 16; religious, 5, 32, 72–74

Imitation of Life, 77

"Industry and Hypocrisy" (Almodóvar), 75

Instituto de Cine, 59

Jackson, Michael, 150

Jameson, Fredric, 116

Johnny Guitar (Ray), 62, 63

Kael, Pauline, 44, 53, 132

Kazan, Elia: *Splendor in the Grass,* 37, 125, 150

Kika (Almodóvar), 80–85; gender in, 82;

mediated reality in, 83–84; music in, 81; narrative in, 10; NC-17 rating of, 84; plot of, 80–81, 82–83, 84; production of, 68, 80; rape in, 80–81, 83–84; reception of, 80, 84–85, 93; setting of, 68, 80, 81–82, 84; sexual identity in, 83

Kinder, Marsha, 38, 54; on *All about My Mother,* 103; *Blood Cinema,* 30–31; on *The Flower of My Secret,* 92; on *High Heels,* 77; interview with Almodóvar, 131–44; on melodrama, 6; on *Tie Me Up! Tie Me Down!,* 73

KIO Towers (Madrid), 98

Kitsch: aesthetics of, 36–37; in Francoist culture, 5; religious, 37, 58, 72

Labyrinth of Passions (Almodóvar), 4, 16, 26–29; budget of, 26; camp in, 27–28; identity confusion in, 28–29; Madrid in, 17; *la movida madrileña* in, 28, 50; plotting of, 26–27; screwball comedy in, 26, 28, 68

Lajusticia, Santiago, 80

Lake, Veronica, 125

Lampreave, Chus: in *Dark Habits,* 33; in *The Flower of My Secret,* 86; in *Matador,* 50, 51; in *What Have I Done to Deserve This?,* 3, 39; in *Women on the Verge of a Nervous Breakdown,* 60

Lauren Films, 60

Law of Desire (Almodóvar), 52–59, 107; autobiography in, 11, 54, 55, 59, 135–36; awards of, 59; family in, 103, 142; financial support for, 53–54; gay identity in, 53, 56, 59; human voice in, 57; incest in, 137, 139; international release of, 53; international success of, 131, 143; Kael on, 132; lesbianism in, 103; Madrid in, 46, 55, 56, 58; *la movida madrileña* in, 56; movie watching in, 140; music of, 57–58; plot of, 54–55; production of, 52; reception of, 59, 131, 143; recycling in, 55–56, 126; religious discourse in, 59, 141; sexual identity in, 46, 55–58; sexuality of, 74; spectator response in, 138; success of, 52; transition to democracy in, 56

Leavitt, David, 43

ing discourse, 38; subversive qualities of, 6, 32; in *Talk to Her,* 111; in *What Have I Done to Deserve This?,* 29, 87; in *Women on the Verge of a Nervous Breakdown,* 88; women's use of, 29–30. *See also* Heroines, melodramatic

Melodrama, Hollywood, 31, 38; Almodóvar's use of, 9, 51, 63, 77, 134

Méndez-Leite, Fernando, 54

Migration: in Almodóvar's films, 38; in *Dark Habits,* 29; and nostalgia, 41; in *What Have I Done to Deserve This?,* 30, 40; women's, 30

Miguel, Fabio de. *See* MacNamara, Fanny

Mildred Pierce, 77

Mills, Hayley, 150

Ministry of Culture: Miró law, 45, 53; subsidies for Almodóvar, 45, 60, 132

Mira, Alberto, 27, 56

Miramax (distributor), 75

Mise-en-scène: of Almodóvar's films, 143; of *Dark Habits,* 35–36; of *Matador,* 51, 68; of *What Have I Done to Deserve This?,* 39, 41; of *Women on the Verge of a Nervous Breakdown,* 66

Mitchum, Robert, 151

Molina, Angela, 95, 96

Molina, Micky: in *Law of Desire,* 54

Molina, Miguel de, 41

Monroe, Marilyn, 58, 141

Montesinos, Francisco, 48

Montiel, Sara, 124, 125

Motherhood: and creativity, 102, 103, 104; in Spanish culture, 142

Mothers: in *All about My Mother,* 102, 103–4; in Almodóvar's films, 142–43; in *The Flower of My Secret,* 100; in *High Heels,* 77, 79; in *Matador,* 142

Motion Picture Association of America (MPAA), classification system of, 75, 84–85, 114

La movida madrileña: Almodóvar and, 18, 105; in *Dark Habits,* 29; in *Labyrinth of Passions,* 28, 50; in *Law of Desire,* 56; *pasotismo* in, 18, 97; passing of, 66; in *Pepi, Luci, Bom,* 23–24, 50. *See also* Madrid

Muerte en la carretera (Almodóvar), 15

Murnau, F. W.: *Sunrise,* 112–13

My Fair Lady (film), 34

Nandorfy, Martha J., 72

National Film School (Madrid), 15

Negulesco, Jean, 62

Neorealism, Italian, 2, 13, 38, 134–35; in Spanish cinema, 41, 135

Neri, Francesca, 94

New York Film Critics' Circle, 67

Nieves Conde, José Antonio: *Surcos,* 31, 39

The Night of the Hunter, 151

Night of the Living Dead (Romero), 70

No Orchids for Miss Blandish (Clowes), 150

Nostalgia: and migration, 41; for Spanish past, 128

Nymphomaniacs in Almodóvar's films, 17

Opus Dei (Catholic organization), 47, 50, 142. See also Ecclesiastic establishment

Palma, Rossy de: in *The Flower of My Secret,* 86; in *Kika,* 80; in *Women on the Verge of a Nervous Breakdown,* 60

Paredes, Marisa: in *All about My Mother,* 100; in *Dark Habits,* 33, 80; in *The Flower of My Secret,* 80, 85, 87; in *High Heels,* 76, 80; in *Talk to Her,* 110

Paris, Texas (Wenders), 141, 150

Parody, in Almodóvar's films, 133

Partido Popular (Spain), 97–98; Almodóvar and, 128; fall of, 115

Pascual, Cristina Sánchez, 22; in *Dark Habits,* 33

Pasolini, Pier Paolo, 13

Pasotismo, 18; Almodóvar's, 97

Patria chica (community), 3, 90

Patriarchy: in *All about My Mother,* 103; in *High Heels,* 79; melodramatic view of, 32; in Spanish culture, 45; in *What Have I Done to Deserve This?,* 42

Patty Diphusa (Almodóvar), 7, 14, 90

Peña, Caldela, 101

Pepi, Luci, Bom, and Other Girls on the

Sexo va, sexo viene (Almodóvar), 15
Sexual identity: in Kika, 83; in Law of
   Desire, 46, 55–58; in Matador, 46–47.
   See also Gender identity
Sexuality: bullfighting and, 49–50; in Live
   Flesh, 96; relation to death, 47; of Tie
   Me Up! Tie Me Down!, 74
Shepard, Sam: Fool for Love, 151
Siegal, Don: Invasion of the Body Snatch-
   ers, 70
Simmons, Jean, 125
Sirk, Douglas, 32, 89; melodramas of,
   63, 134
Sisters (De Palma), 150
Sisters, cinematic, 150
Siva, Eva, 22, 24
Smith, Paul Julian, 66; on Iberian char-
   acter, 52; on melodrama, 6; on Tie Me
   Up! Tie Me Down!, 72; on What Have
   I Done to Deserve This?, 40
Soap operas, radio, 3
Social reality, in Almodóvar's films, 91, 92
Soler Leal, Amparo, 44
Songs, Latin American, 65, 92
Sound, juxtaposition with image, 16
"Soy infeliz" (song), 65
Spain: internal migrations in, 4, 30; urban
   versus rural, 90, 116. See also Culture,
   Spanish
Spain, Francoist: backwardness of, 2–4;
   ecclesiastic establishment in, 34, 127;
   folkloric culture of, 3, 5, 68; geocultural dynamic of, 89; in Live Flesh, 95,
   97; marginalization of, 13, 105; versus
   modern Spain, 90; nostalgia for, 128;
   popular culture of, 121; religious iconography of, 73; suspension of rights
   in, 95; traditional culture of, 43. See
   also Francoism
Spain, post-Franco: in Bad Education,
   122, 123; cinema in, 131–32; cultural
   genealogy of, 78; cultural heterogeneity
   of, 38; ecclesiastical establishment in,
   132; freedom of expression in, 14; gays
   in, 29; gender identity in, 29; geocultural repositioning of, 17; in Live Flesh,
   94; modernization in, 43, 52, 63, 66, 68,

116; morality of, 50; political culture of,
   97; social reality of, 91; Spanish cinema
   in, 131–32; versus traditional Spain, 90;
   transnational community of, 92, 104;
   underclass of, 98; women in, 29. See
   also Transition to democracy, Spanish
Spanish Association of Film Directors, 59
Spectator experience: in Almodóvar's
   films, 133, 136, 140, 141; in Law of
   Desire, 138
Splendor in the Grass (Kazan), 37, 125,
   150
Stanton, Harry Dean, 150
Stanwyck, Barbara, 125, 149
Star (magazine), 20
Stella Dallas, 77
Storytelling, in Almodóvar's films, 2, 9,
   10–11, 38
Strauss, Frédéric, 99
Streetcar Named Desire (Williams),
   100–101, 102, 104
Sturges, Preston, 26
Suárez, Gonzalo, 40, 44
Super 8 movies, Almodóvar's, 2, 15–16, 25
Swanson, Gloria, 105

Talk to Her (Almodóvar), 106–14; and All
   about My Mother, 106; bullfighting in,
   109, 110, 111; dance in, 107, 108, 109,
   113–14; film-within-a-film of, 112, 149;
   flashbacks in, 109; gay relationships
   in, 109; gender identity in, 47, 108–9;
   human body in, 113–14; human voice
   in, 107; loneliness in, 114; male characters of, 46; melodrama in, 111; music
   in, 109, 110–11; narrative of, 10, 110,
   113; Oscar for, 114; plot of, 107; pre-
   text of, 106; rape in, 74; reception of,
   114; self-referentiality in, 64; Shrinking
   Lover episode, 112–13; structure of,
   106, 109–10, 149
Tashlin, Frank, 13
Taylor, Elizabeth, 141
Terrorism, Basque, 128
Tesauro Films, 37
Therese Raquin (Carné), 126
Thompson, David, 77–78

63, 66; melodrama in, 63, 69, 88; melodramatic heroines of, 60; mise-en-scène
of, 66; music in, 65; narrative of, 10, 60;
Oscar nomination for, 67; plot of, 61–62;
screwball comedy in, 68; voices in, 64
Women's liberation, in *What Have I Done
to Deserve This?*, 140
Wood, Natalie, 150

Yarza, Alejandro, 19, 72, 74, 89
Youth culture: international, 17–18;
Madrid's, 16–17

Zavattini, Cesare, 134
Zunzunegui, Santos, 23
Zurbarán, Francisco, 32

Marvin D'Lugo is professor of Spanish and screen studies at Clark University in Worcester, Massachusetts. He is the author of *The Films of Carlos Saura: The Practice of Seeing* and *Guide to the Cinema of Spain.*

Books in the series Contemporary Film Directors

Pedro Almodóvar
  Marvin D'Lugo

Joel and Ethan Coen
  R. Barton Palmer

Claire Denis
  Judith Mayne

Nelson Pereira dos Santos
  Darlene J. Sadlier

Wong Kar-wai
  Peter Brunette

Abbas Kiarostami
  Mehrnaz Saeed-Vafa and Jonathan Rosenbaum

Chris Marker
  Nora Alter

Edward Yang
  John Anderson

The University of Illinois Press
is a founding member of the
Association of American University Presses.

Composed in 10/13 New Caledonia
with Helvetica Neue Extended display
by Barbara Evans
at the University of Illinois Press
Designed by Paula Newcomb
Manufactured by Thomson-Shore, Inc.

University of Illinois Press
1325 South Oak Street
Champaign, IL 61820-6903
www.press.uillinois.edu